The Enticement
of the Forbidden

Protecting Your Marriage

Personal Study and Discussion Guide

Judy Starr

The Enticement of the Forbidden
Protecting Your Marriage
Personal Study and Discussion Guide

Published by
LifeConneXions
A ministry of Campus Crusade for Christ
375 Highway 74 South, Suite A
Peachtree City, GA 30269

Cover by Larry Smith and Associates
Printed in the United States of America
ISBN 1-56399-221-3

Unless otherwise indicated, Scripture quotations are from the *New American Standard Bible*, ©1960, 1962, 1963, 1968, 1971, 1972, 1973, 1975, 1977, 1995 by the Lockman Foundation, La Habra, California.

Scripture quotations designated NIV are from the *New International Version*, © 1973, 1978, 1984 by the International Bible Society. Published by Zondervan Bible Publishers, Grand Rapids, Michigan.

Scripture quotations designated TLB are from *The Living Bible*, © 1971 by Tyndale House Publishers, Wheaton, Illinois.

Contents

This study guide is dedicated to my precious Mom,

Dottie Antosh

Mom, you are perfectly described in Matthew 5:6: "Blessed are those who hunger and thirst for righteousness, for they shall be satisfied." What a privilege to have a mother who passionately thirsts for God and His Word. I am indeed blessed. I love you so much!

The Transformation Process

As I looked down at my wedding ring, my heart ached to be with the man I thought I loved—but he wasn't my husband! So with my heart feeling raw and broken, I chose to leave this man and return home. At that point a hardened, insensitive spirit toward God lay cold inside my soul. But in my desperation to know His presence and peace once again, I determined to hang in there and do whatever it took to soften my hardened heart of stone into a heart of flesh (Ezekiel 11:19). And as I started choosing obedience, God graciously began to tenderize and remold my heart and mind again. I won't tell you it was easy, because that process often felt quite painful! But the end results were worth every moment of the pain required in order to restore my relationship with God and with my husband.

Change is never easy. Yet without change, nothing will grow. Unless the ground is plowed up and overturned, the soil can never be ready to produce crops. The same is true for our lives. Unless we are willing to look into our hearts and overturn those hard, unbroken areas, we will remain in the same ruts and destructive patterns the rest of our earthly days. And the longer we stay that way, the harder it becomes to change!

I still have moments during my time in God's presence when He points His finger at an area in my life that needs changing. When that happens, I often feel tempted to get up and end my time with Him early. But I choose to stay and confront those areas because I know that as I do, He will transform my life and root out the places that need changing so that I can continue to grow.

Although our lives and the world around us constantly change, God and His Word never do. Isaiah writes, *"The grass withers, the flower fades, but the word of our God stands forever"* (Isaiah 40:8). What a blessing to have a Rock upon which we can depend completely, without fail. *"The Rock! His work is perfect, for all His ways are just; a God of faithfulness and without injustice, righteous and upright is He"* (Deuteronomy 32:4). *"The Lord is my rock and my fortress and my deliverer, my God, my rock, in whom I take refuge"* (Psalm 18:2).

Because God and His Word never change, He alone must form the foundation for all we think, believe, and do. That's why you will find so much Scripture throughout *The Enticement of the Forbidden*, and why we will spend time learning from His Word in this study guide. If God said it, it's true, and I'm going to stake my life on it!

For God to truly transform our lives, we must confront our propensity to sin and acknowledge that we can all fall into any sin known to man. That knowledge drives us to come to the Lord each day. It was only when I started coming to the Lord in desperation every morning that I began to witness the miraculous changes in my heart that only He can make. He also began opening my eyes to things in His Word that now form the truths you will read about as you go through *The Enticement of the Forbidden* and this accompanying Personal Study and Discussion Guide. I believe in these truths with all my heart because I have seen in my life and in others' lives the transformation that comes when we follow His Word.

So let's begin this lifelong journey with the Lord by laying a solid foundation so that our lives will become more and more like Christ, shining with His holiness, radiating *"the peace of God, which surpasses all comprehension"* (Philippians 4:7). Such a life is only found in Him!

Using this Study

T hank goodness God didn't create us and then leave us to stumble through life alone! He loves to meet with us and yearns to guide us with His wisdom so that we can become more and more like Christ.

But there are no shortcuts to spiritual growth. That's why I'm excited that you are using this study guide along with reading the book. This daily study will help you apply the truths that you are learning from *The Enticement of the Forbidden* into your own life and marriage. As you dig into His Word and allow Him to transform you, a depth of spiritual life you never dreamed possible will begin to take place. *"For I am confident of this very thing, that He who began a good work in you will perfect it until the day of Christ Jesus"* (Philippians 1:6).

This study can be used in two ways. First, as a personal, daily study, it will help you apply the concepts from *The Enticement of the Forbidden* to your own life, guiding you as you grow deeper in God's Word and protect your marriage. Second, this study guide can also be used with a small group of women. In the back of this book are discussion questions that correspond with each week's lessons. Your discussion group will meet once a week to discuss what you have been learning. However, your answers in the Personal Study will only be addressed in a general sense, so please open your heart honestly before the Lord as you answer the daily questions.

Plan to do these daily lessons during the week, and bring what you have learned to the weekly discussion group. If you do not plan to meet with a discussion group, consider adapting the Discussion Guide as a conversation between you and your accountability partner. If you will not be meeting with anyone, then turn to the Discussion Guide at the end of each week's lessons and go through the questions and material on your own. There is new material in the Discussion Guide that you definitely won't want to miss!

The Personal Study

The Personal Study plan includes five lessons per week. Study one lesson per day, either during your Quiet Time with God or at another time during the day when you can focus on God's Word.

Each daily lesson includes several parts. They are designed to help you focus on God, learn what the Bible says on the subject covered, and apply the truths to your life. These are the lesson components:

Reading

This is the chapter(s) in *The Enticement of the Forbidden* covered in the lesson. Be sure you have read these pages in the book before you work on the lesson. If you read the chapter at an earlier time, reviewing it would be helpful before you prepare to do the lesson.

Spending Time with God

This is a short devotional time that will help you focus on God before you start your lesson.

Evaluating My Views

These questions will help you consider your current views on the topic to be studied. It is essential to be honest about your opinions so that you can address any changes the Lord may want you to make.

Finding God's Perspective

This section will guide you into the Scriptures to help you see what God says about the topic. This is the heart of your study. There's nothing better than digging into His Word!

Checking My Heart

This part of the lesson takes what God says and helps you apply the principles specifically to your unique situation. This is where you examine your heart concerning the issues raised and look at how God may desire you to change.

Allowing God to Transform Me

After learning what God says about the subject and how that affects your life, it's time to implement the principles you have learned. This section is where your study allows God to begin transforming your life.

As you work through the lessons, keep a prayer list in your study guide. You could use the inside front cover to record your requests, or keep a separate piece of paper in your workbook. This will become a great encouragement as you see God's answers to your prayers. Write down requests, answers to prayer, Scripture references that apply to your prayers, and praises to God. Be sure to date your entries so that you can keep track of when your prayers are answered. A suggestion is to make a chart like this one:

Prayer Request	Date	Prayer Request	Date

If you are also participating in a discussion group, include a section for the prayer requests and praises that come from your time with the women in your study group.

Also, designate a section of your prayer chart for your accountability partnership. (In *The Enticement of the Forbidden*, you will learn about setting up accountability.) Pray for your accountability partner's needs regularly. And don't forget to include a section of prayer requests for your husband!

The Discussion Guide

When you meet once a week with your discussion group, you will talk with other women about what you have been learning from the daily lessons. This will be done by going through questions found in the Discussion Guide. God calls us to learn from one another, so receiving the wisdom, viewpoints, and encouragement of other women is vital to achieving maximum spiritual growth. You will find that these sessions also help you stick with the changes you are making in your marriage relationship and in your commitment to God.

If you are the facilitator for a discussion group, you will find the Discussion Guide toward the end of this book. Each week's discussion includes material for your use in guiding your group time. Study this material before leading each weekly session. Your group members do not need to turn to these pages because you will read the questions and added material to them aloud. As the leader, frequently emphasize that all personal information shared within the group must be held in *strictest confidence* by all other group members. Also, remind the women that they will want to be careful about sharing with others any personal and private matters concerning their husbands. The issue of respecting and honoring one another in our marriage is vital, even if the marriage is a difficult one. Therefore, encourage them to consider talking with their husband and, if possible, receiving his permission beforehand to share such things.

Our precious Lord loves us so much and desires to transform us so that we *"may be filled with the knowledge of His will in all spiritual wisdom and understanding"* (Colossians 1:9). What a privilege we have to study His Word and to know God! And as we allow Him to change us, we then experience His fullness and His peace—something that is very precious to me since I stood on the threshold of marital disaster.

As you go through this study, *"I pray that the eyes of your heart may be enlightened, so that you may know what is the hope of His calling, what are the riches of the glory of His inheritance in the saints, and what is the surpassing greatness of His power toward us who believe"* (Ephesians 1:18,19).

Personal Study Guide

Personal Study
Week One

Understanding Our Problem and God's Perspective

Lesson 1
"We Have a Problem"

Note: These daily lessons are for your eyes only. For group discussion times the Discussion Guide, found in the back of this book, asks a new set of questions. So please be as transparent as possible in answering these daily questions.

Reading: chapters 1 and 2.

Spending Time with God

Oh, the heartache and destruction we can cause in our own life and in the lives of those around us when we choose to live according to our selfish desires! How desperately we need God's wisdom and guidance. Proverbs 3:5,6 says, *"Trust in the Lord with all your heart and do not lean on your own understanding. In all your ways acknowledge Him, and He will make your paths straight."* To begin your time in this study, place your heart in God's hands. Read those verses again, thinking about the instructions we are to follow. Then commit this study time to God. Ask the Lord to guide you as you read His Word.

Evaluating My Views

In the space below, write out your perspective of what your marriage relationship is like right now. Especially make note of any ways that emotional and/or physical infidelity may have touched your marriage.

Finding God's Perspective

1. Read Hebrews 13:4. How are God's standards in marriage different than the world's standards?

2. Read 1 Thessalonians 4:1–5. What directions does God give us concerning moral purity?

3. Christian author and clinical psychologist Dr. Willard Harley calls infidelity "the greatest threat to your marriage."[1] How does this quote apply to the Hebrews 13 and 1 Thessalonian 4 passages and to marriages today?

Checking My Heart

According to *Psychology Today* magazine, "Half the American couples over 40 years of age have experienced extramarital affairs at some point."[2] But it doesn't end there. More and more older women are also choosing to follow their feelings rather than their vows.

1. In what ways can a woman choose to commit emotional infidelity even if she hasn't committed physical infidelity?

2. List areas in your life—work relationships, friendships, neighborhood contacts—that could present opportunities toward developing either emotional or physical ties to another man.

3. What steps could you take to avoid compromising situations?

Allowing God to Transform Me

God loves us so much and wants only that which is for our good. As we choose to follow Him, we begin to see how every area of our lives can reflect His purity, and we also experience His peace. As you begin to delve into this study of *The Enticement of the Forbidden*, ask God to help you become more sensitive to His standards for your marriage. If a situation exists in your life where emotional or physical infidelity may have already become a danger point, ask the Lord to give you His perspective on keeping your marriage pure.

Lesson 2
"God's Perspective on Marriage and Wives"

Reading: chapter 3.

Spending Time with God

God tells us, *"The wise woman builds her house, but the foolish tears it down with her own hands"* (Proverbs 14:1). As you think about this verse, ask God to show you what kind of foundation you have for your "life house." Think through the major decisions you have made over the last week. Was each decision made on the basis of God's Word or on what you thought was right?

Evaluating My Views

1. How would you describe your commitment level to your marriage?

2. Write a paragraph on your views about your role as a wife.

3. How does the world's view on how a wife is to relate to her husband differ from your views? How are they the same?

Finding God's Perspective

Because God loves us so much, He gave us clear instructions on how we are designed to function and live. When we disregard these precepts, problems always develop. Psychologist Dr. James Dobson says, "We are all governed by a moral code that cannot be violated without inevitable consequences."[3]

1. After reading Mark 10:6–9, describe in your own words the bond God wants to see in a marriage.

2. Read Ephesians 5:21–33. Write down God's marriage principles for husbands. Then write down God's marriage principles for wives.

Christian author Susan Foh writes: "Wives are to *submit themselves* (reflexive); their submission is voluntary, self-imposed. It is part of their obedience to the Lord; the Lord is the one who commands it, not the husband."[4]

3. What difference does it make to a marriage when the spouses submit to God first?

Checking My Heart

Mike Mason, in his book *The Mystery of Marriage*, calls marriage "an unrelenting guerrilla warfare against selfishness."[5]

1. On the scale below, mark from 1 to 10 how selfish you think you are in your marriage relationship. Do you frequently think about how your marriage can fulfill you and make you happy, or do you usually act out of self-sacrifice and commitment to your husband?

1		10
Self-sacrificing		Selfish

2. How does 1 Peter 3:1–4 apply to your relationship with your husband?

3. In what ways can you be an example of Proverbs 31:10–12 in your marriage?

Allowing God to Transform Me

Turn your husband over to God's care. Thank God for your husband's positive characteristics. Now thank Him for your husband's weaknesses and ask God to help you show respect toward your spouse, exhibiting a gentle and quiet spirit.

Lesson 3
"God's Perspective on Affairs and Divorce"

Note: Remember, all these daily lessons are for your eyes only.

Reading: Review chapter 3 from the section titled "God's Perspective on Affairs" to the end.

Spending Time with God

As you read the following verse, ask God to reveal any ways that you may have a casual attitude toward keeping your marriage pure and sacred. Lay those before the Lord and thank Him that He can enable you to change these attitudes or actions. *"Marriage should be honored by all, and the marriage bed kept pure, for God will judge the adulterer and all the sexually immoral"* (Hebrews 13:4, NIV).

Evaluating My Views

1. What kind of emotional response does the phrase "she's having an affair" elicit from you?

2. How do you feel about Charles Colson's statement: "Even under the worst of circumstances—adultery, abuse, and abandonment—God does not command divorce. He merely permits it. And divorce is always a trauma. In this age of no-fault divorce, Christians ought to do everything possible to protect their marriages."[6]

Finding God's Perspective

There is definitely something enticing about the forbidden. Just ask Eve. The one thing she was denied in the midst of paradise—the fruit of the tree—became an alluring temptation. And the results of her choice to disobey God brought disaster (Genesis 3)! Sin will always be tempting. That's why we so desperately need to know *God's* perspective—because He knows the *results* of our choices.

1. How does God describe an immoral woman in Proverbs 5:3–6?

2. According to Proverbs 6:27–29,32, what is the result of a person's choice of adultery?

3. Looking at Malachi 2:16 and Mark 10:9, what does God teach us concerning divorce?

Checking My Heart

1. What are some of the consequences that could occur if you ever decided to divorce?

2. In a study on marriage and divorce, 92 percent of the couples who remained together in spite of serious marital troubles later said they were "glad they were still together."[7] Why do you think they were happier?

Most of us think that because we are Christian our marriage will be "Christian." But a godly marriage doesn't just happen because we go to church and even read our Bibles. It takes work, and it requires building safeguards against the onslaughts that inevitably will occur. We should fear the ease with which we can so easily fall to temptation and sin. God warns us, *"How blessed is the man who fears always, but he who hardens his heart will fall into calamity"* (Proverbs 28:14).

3. What examples can you give from your own experience that show the truth of that verse?

Allowing God to Transform Me

Ask God to give you His perspective on affairs and divorce. If you have feelings of discontent in your marriage, turn those over to God. (He already knows your heart.) Ask Him to help you persevere through troubled times, remembering that He can restore your love.

Lesson 4
"How Can a Christian Woman Fall into Infidelity?"

Reading: chapter 4.

Spending Time with God

Temptation leading away from the Lord always looks exciting and enticing. That's why we're tempted! Yet the result brings only long-term sorrow and destruction. God tells us that we are fools when we enjoy sin. *"A fool finds pleasure in evil conduct, but a man of understanding delights in wisdom"* (Proverbs 10:23, NIV). Examine your heart before God, asking Him to reveal where sin is a pleasure to you. Ask Him to help you desire to be pure and wise in all areas of your life, especially in those that God reveals as impure.

Evaluating My Views

Dr. Shirley Glass says about some spouses: "For them, part of the passion and excitement of an affair is the lying and getting away with something forbidden."[8]

1. In what ways is this like your life?

Dr. Scott Haltzman writes about unfaithful partners: "For an overwhelming majority of spouses who cheat—80 percent—the reason is not sexual. Most simply seek validation, warmth, understanding, or love."[9]

2. Which areas do you feel are most needy in your relationship with your husband? (Check those that apply.)

   ❑ Need for his respect and validation
   ❑ Need for warmth and love
   ❑ Desire for greater understanding
   ❑ Desire for his attention, to feel important
   ❑ Need for time alone together
   ❑ Desire for excitement

3. How does your daily schedule contribute to your pleasure or dissatisfaction with your marriage?

Finding God's Perspective

1. Isaiah 30:1 says, *"'Woe to the rebellious children,' declares the Lord, 'Who execute a plan, but not Mine, and make an alliance, but not of My Spirit, in order to add sin to sin.'"* What is God saying about the person who is determined to do things her way rather than God's way?

2. Rewrite Proverbs 9:13–18, putting the situation into a modern setting.

3. How can Psalm 20:1–5 give you hope for how God will help you overcome any difficulties you are having in your marriage or your life?

Checking My Heart

Attraction to another man can happen to anyone at any age. This infatuation most often begins with someone who meets your desires for warmth, validation, and love. Your self-image receives strokes—someone finds you attractive and desirable! Suddenly, you experience feelings you don't want to lose. There is a sense of freshness in the excitement of this secret infatuation.

1. In what ways have you found this to be true in your life?

2. What steps will you take to avoid situations in which you are prone to temptation in this area?

Allowing God to Transform Me

Read Psalm 1:1–3 *"How blessed is the man who does not walk in the counsel of the wicked, nor stand in the path of sinners, nor sit in the seat of scoffers! But his delight is in the law of the Lord, and in His law he meditates day and night. He will be like a tree firmly planted by streams of water, which yields its fruit in its season and its leaf does not wither; and in whatever he does, he prospers."* Seeing how easily choices of sin can snowball, ask God to continue revealing your heart. He is the only One who can give you the power to change. Ask Him to help you follow His path and to delight in His wisdom.

Lesson 5
"Opportunities Everywhere"

Reading: Glance back through the main headings in chapters 1–4.

Spending Time with God

God listens to those who truly turn to Him. Read Psalm 51:1-10. Tell God how David's feelings reflect your own. Let God know how sorry you are for any indiscretions you may have committed against your husband. Ask Him to give you a clean heart and a steadfast spirit.

Evaluating My Views

1. How have your opinions about infidelity changed since you began this study?

2. How do you think our culture has influenced you to hold wrong views about marriage and unfaithfulness?

3. In what ways could these wrong views lead to disastrous consequences?

Finding God's Perspective

1. Read Colossians 3:12–15. How can you apply these verses to your relationship with your husband?

2. Now go on to read verses 16,17 of Colossians 3. What principles can you take from these verses that can help you manage any difficulties in your marriage or help to strengthen your marriage?

Checking My Heart

1. Look in the book at the scenario that led me (Judy) to attraction toward Eric. (It's found in the beginning of chapter 4 up to the heading "How Women Get Into Problems.") What choices did I make that allowed me to get to the point of falling for another man?

2. Did you see yourself in any of the marriage scenarios described in chapter 4 in the section titled "How Women Get Into Problems"? Describe the similarities.

3. Describe the process you will undertake to make your choices more godly and supportive to your marriage.

Allowing God to Transform Me

Spend time asking God to help you make the choices you listed above.

Note: If you will *not* be meeting with a discussion group or with another person to go through the Discussion Guide, please turn now to page 118 and go through the questions and new material for Week One as if it were another daily lesson. You won't want to miss the additional insights found there!

Personal Study
Week Two

Choosing Marriage Over
Temptation

Lesson 1
"The Results of Our Choices"

Note: Remember, all these daily lessons are for your eyes only. For group discussion times the Discussion Guide, found in the back of this book, asks a new set of questions. So please be as transparent as possible in answering these daily questions.

Reading: chapter 5

Spending Time with God

God is so amazingly patient with sinful humans because He loves us so much and desires to lead us out of our foolish ways. Romans 2:4 says, *"Or do you think lightly of the riches of His kindness and tolerance and patience, not knowing that the kindness of God leads you to repentance?"* Think of ways that God has been kind to you. Consider areas such as health, material possessions, family, jobs, Christian friends, and church support. Thank God for His kindness toward you.

Evaluating My Views

1. Jesus said, *"These things I speak in the world so that they may have My joy made full in themselves"* (John 17:13).[1] How does it make you feel to know that God desires for you to experience an abundant life full of peace and joy?

2. The ability to leave sin and to change your actions (repentance) is a gift from God. How does this make you feel about choices you may be making to continue disobeying Him?[2]

When we choose to continue in sin (disobedience to God) and refuse to change our ways, our conscience can become hardened to God's will until we no longer even hear His voice. And we will reap the full consequences of our actions.

3. Proverbs 29:1 says, *"A man who hardens his neck after much reproof will suddenly be broken beyond remedy."* How could that principle apply to a woman who refuses to follow God's instructions to flee immorality?

Finding God's Perspective

The bottom line for infidelity—or *any* sin—always comes back to the choices we make. And with each choice, we decide whether to follow God or to listen to Satan's temptations. God loves us so much that He sent His Son Jesus to die for us. Satan hates us so much that he wants only that which destroys our lives and our futures. He *wants* our marriages to crumble and our ministries to disintegrate in shame. His desire is to steal and kill and destroy us, and he prowls around like a starving lion awaiting even the smallest opportunity to devour our lives (1 Peter 5:8). He's not called "our adversary" for nothing!

There are only two paths we may follow. In the chart below, contrast the results of choosing Satan's way versus God's way. Think of examples from your life, what you have seen around you, or what you believe may happen.

Verses	Results of Choosing Satan's Way	Results of Choosing God's Way
1 Peter 5:8–10		
John 10:10		
Proverbs 1:28–33		

Checking My Heart

The vows you made on your wedding day were made to God first, then to your husband. Keep this in mind as you answer the following questions.

1. What do you remember about the vows you made to your husband on your wedding day? Write out as much as possible.

2. What do these vows mean to you today? Be honest.

3. We know that God's will for us is always for our good. Read Numbers 30:1,2. How does this verse change your view of your marriage vows?

Allowing God to Transform Me

The Bible tells us to *"offer to God a sacrifice of thanksgiving and pay your vows to the Most High; call upon Me in the day of trouble; I shall rescue you, and you will honor Me"* (Psalm 50:14,15). Call upon God to help you remain true to your marriage vows. Whatever failings you have done are now in the past. Resolve to start anew, keeping your vows sacred from here on.

His Word tells us to offer *"a sacrifice of thanksgiving"* to Him, whether our situation is easy or difficult. Thank Him for your marriage, trusting that He will strengthen you to remain faithful as you call upon Him.

Lesson 2
"Be Honest with Yourself"

Reading: chapter 6.

Spending Time with God

God tells us, *"The heart is more deceitful than all else and is desperately sick; who can understand it? I, the Lord, search the heart, I test the mind, even to give to each man according to his ways, according to the results of his deeds"* (Jeremiah 17:9,10). Ask God to show you what is truly in your heart as you go through this lesson.

Evaluating My Views

1. What do you think of the phrase: "Never underestimate the power of attraction"?

2. How have you seen yourself or someone you know rationalize feelings of attraction toward someone else?

3. How have you witnessed the tendency in human nature to always want more?

Finding God's Perspective

1. One problem we face in our marriage relationships is not being honest with ourselves about our own failings and problems. God's Holy Spirit can help us see ourselves as we truly are. Ask Him to help you in this first step to building a godly marriage: Be honest with yourself.

2. Read Proverbs 12:20. How does this verse apply to emotional and physical infidelity?

3. In Romans 1:21, what process does Paul describe concerning people who keep on sinning?

4. Describe how you can be honest with yourself when confronted with a temptation or an attraction to another man.

Checking My Heart

We can never be truly honest with ourselves until we allow God to reveal those areas in our hearts that may not be readily apparent.

1. List any areas in which you have difficulty with temptation in your marriage. This could include attitudes and thoughts.

2. Read Psalm 5:1–7. What actions do these verses give to help you open your heart to God?

3. Ask God for His perspective on the areas of temptation that you listed in question 1. Then lay those before Him and ask for His strength to resist the enemy and to make godly choices.

Allowing God to Transform Me

Use Psalm 26:2 in a prayer, asking God to continue searching your heart: *"Examine me, O Lord, and try me; test my mind and my heart."* Christ tells us that His grace is sufficient (2 Corinthians 12:9), so ask Christ to strengthen you in your weaknesses. He yearns for us to depend on Him.

Lesson 3
"Be Honest with God"

Reading: In chapter 6, review the section titled "Be Honest with God."

Spending Time with God

Only God can change our perspective to see life through His eyes. Each day, we must let Him rearrange our priorities, make us less selfish, and mold us to be like Christ. This, in turn, *greatly* impacts our marriage. Christian author and speaker Cynthia Heald says, "A wife rightly related to her Lord will be a wife rightly related to her husband."[3]

God tells us that the person with whom He fellowships is the one "*who is humble and contrite of spirit and who trembles at My word*" (Isaiah 66:2). Do you meet with Him each day, understanding that the quality of every single relationship in your life is dependent upon your relationship with God? Take a few moments in prayer to give God first place in your life again.

Evaluating My Views

1. Describe things that cause your heart to become hardened and insensitive to the Lord.

2. Write down the times in your daily schedule when you spend time in God's Word and in His presence.

3. How do you think spending daily, meaningful time in the Bible and in God's presence will keep your spirit tender and sensitive to His leading?

Finding God's Perspective

1. What does Psalm 119:9–11 say are the results of maintaining honesty with God?

2. According to Psalm 119:162–165, what actions keep our heart sensitive to the Lord?

Because I (Judy) believe this with all my heart, let me say it again: I am convinced that *the most critical element in protecting your marriage is your personal time alone with God.* It is irreplaceable; there are no substitutes.

3. In what ways do you need to change your attitude about spending time with the Lord every day?

Checking My Heart

Read Psalm 86:5 to find a wonderful description of God. Because of God's goodness, love, and forgiveness, we can lay all areas of our life at His feet and commit again to maintaining honesty with Him through daily time in His Word and presence.

1. What areas in your life have you kept hidden from the Lord?

2. After studying the verses from Psalm 119 above, what difference will these verses make in your daily schedule so that you can keep a sensitive and tender heart to the Lord?

Allowing God to Transform Me

Read Deuteronomy 10:12,13 and ask God to make this true for your commitment to Him.

Lesson 4
"Be Honest with Your Husband"

Note: Remember, all these daily lessons are for your eyes only.

Reading: In chapter 6, review the sections titled "Be Honest with Your Husband" and "The No Secrets Policy."

Spending Time with God

Godly marriages don't just happen because one Christian marries another Christian. No marriage is without conflicts, trials, and failures in communication. Yet we know that God is committed to seeing our marriage relationship grow and reflect His love. Godly love *"does not rejoice in unrighteousness, but rejoices with the truth"* (1 Corinthians 13:6). Ask God to give you His perspective on how truthfulness in your marriage demonstrates love.

Evaluating My Views

1. Have you ever felt that sudden tingle of attraction toward another man? What did you do with those feelings? Did you follow God's Word or your feelings?

2. If your heart felt drawn toward another man, and you found yourself repeatedly dwelling on thoughts and pictures of the two of you together, would you tell your husband about your fantasies? Why?

3. Dr. Joyce Brothers writes, "When people who are close are not completely honest with each other, certain avenues of intimacy are invariably cut off."[4] Do you think that having a marriage free of deceit and secrets will enhance trust, closeness, and communication? What might change in your relationship if both of you were totally honest?

Finding God's Perspective

Honesty is an incredible protection for Stottler's and my marriage. The moment I sense that Stottler would be unhappy if he knew what I might do, an enormous red flag pops up in my head. Like most of us, if I think I can hide something, I'm far more likely to give it a try. But immediately exposing the temptation causes it to wither and die.

1. God warns us many times in His Word about the consequences of hiding things and being deceitful. Read the following verses, writing down the main idea and consequence of deceitfulness described in each:

   Jeremiah 17:9,10

   Psalm 36:1–3

2. The following verses speak of the benefits of truthfulness. Write down the benefit you receive for being truthful found in each verse:

   Psalm 15:1,2

   Psalm 51:6,7

3. Now compare the two sets of passages. In a sentence, write out why it is so important for you to be truthful with your husband.

Checking My Heart

1. In what areas do I tend to "fudge" the truth or outright lie to my husband?

2. What is my motive for doing this? How does this secrecy affect our marriage?

3. What are some specific steps I can take to begin implementing the No Secrets Policy in my marriage?

Allowing God to Transform Me

In *The Living Bible*, Ephesians 4:15 says, *"We will lovingly follow the truth at all times—speaking truly, dealing truly, living truly—and so become more and more in every way like Christ."* As we have seen in His Word, God repeatedly calls us to honesty in all areas of our life. Pray and ask the Lord to begin making you willing to do *whatever* He calls you to do for the sake of your marriage. He will always give you the strength to obey.

Lesson 5
"Elements of Restoration"

Reading: In chapter 6, review all sections under "Elements of Restoration."

Spending Time with God

After establishing honesty with yourself, with God, and with your husband, you will begin to see changes in your marriage. To allow God's healing and building to continue, ask Him to reveal where your priorities differ from His found in Matthew 22:37. Ask God to give you His wisdom in setting your priorities.

Evaluating My Views

1. Write out a general schedule of your daily activities. Include the time you spend with God (prayer times, reading the Bible, worshiping, ministry), your husband, your family, and work. Can you honestly say that your priorities in life are God first, then your husband, then your children, and finally your ministry and work?

Answer these questions about any improper relationship or fantasy in which you may be involved now, or how you would respond if this were to happen:

2. If you find yourself caught up in romantic or sexual fantasies toward anyone—fictional or real—how are those fantasies affecting your relationship with your husband?

3. If there is another man with whom you've had an improper relationship—either emotionally or physically—what effect has this had on your marriage?

Finding God's Perspective

The Enticement of the Forbidden gives three elements for restoring a damaged marital relationship and for building barriers against future temptations of infidelity. Let's look at God's perspective for each.

1. Cutting off all contact: Read James 1:14,15. How does staying in contact with a person with whom you have an improper relationship fulfill the process in this verse?

2. Set your priorities: Read Proverbs 2:1–12. How does making God and His Word first priority in your life help you keep all your other priorities right?

3. Rebuild trust: Read Philippians 2:3. How does demonstrating a self-sacrificing love that puts your husband above yourself help repair trust in your marriage that you may have damaged through selfish and secret choices?

Checking My Heart

Whether you have been unfaithful emotionally or physically or may have failed to make your marriage the priority it should be, make a plan to begin restoring and protecting your marriage relationship. Write out what you need to do in each of these areas that apply:

1. Cutting off all contact.

2. Setting your priorities.

3. Rebuilding trust.

Allowing God to Transform Me

God tells us, *"Behold, I am the Lord, the God of all flesh; is anything too difficult for Me?"* (Jeremiah 32:27). Thank God that *He* can give you the strength to follow through on these areas that He has shown you. Ask God to help you reflect His love in your marriage. *Nothing* is too difficult for Him!

Note: If you will *not* be meeting with a discussion group or with another person to go through the Discussion Guide, please turn now to page 121 and go through the questions and new material for Week Two as if it were another daily lesson. You won't want to miss the additional insights found there!

Experiencing the
Transformation of Christ

Lesson 1
"Our Relationship with God"

Reading: chapter 7

Spending Time with God

What gives us the open door to communicate with God? How can we truly come into His presence? Only through Christ's love and forgiveness. *"For You, Lord, are good, and ready to forgive, and abundant in lovingkindness to all who call upon You"* (Psalm 86:5). *"I will sing of the lovingkindness of the Lord forever; to all generations I will make known Your faithfulness with my mouth"* (Psalm 89:1). Meditate on these psalms and write down your thoughts about God's love for you.

Evaluating My Views

We have read about how far God's love reaches to restore us. And as we look at His love, we also confront our own corrupt sinful nature. The root of our sin is always pride. We proudly believe that we don't really need God's help. I don't want to accept that *my* nature is absolutely corrupt. Maybe hers, but not mine. But God says that we *all* fall short of His glory—even those women who seem to be descendants of Pollyanna.

The good news is that we can receive God's transforming power and love into our lives, thereby crucifying pride and establishing a right relationship with Him and with others. Only then can we live out His principles for a fulfilling life and marriage. Honestly ask yourself the following questions:

What roots of pride do I find in my life?

How has pride contributed to problems in my marriage?

Finding God's Perspective

God wants to draw us back to Himself and give us a new heart. He gave us a story in the book of Hosea that illustrates His grace and love lavishly poured upon a wayward wife to draw her back. The wife totally rejected her husband, Hosea, and ran off with other men. Yet Hosea wanted her back and demonstrated unending kindness and forgiveness toward her. In the end, he even had to buy his wife back, which is exactly what Christ did for us!

1. Read Hosea 1:2,3; 2:5–8; 3:1,2. How does this story picture the kind of love God has for us? (Hosea represents God's actions. Adultery is a symbol of our sin against God.)

2. According to 2 Corinthians 5:17, what does God desire to do with your life?

3. Have you put your faith in Christ, receiving His payment for your sins? If you know a specific time, write out when this life-changing decision occurred.

4. What does God tell us in Hebrews 7:25 and 13:5 about how long our relationship with Him will last?

Checking My Heart

1. Whether you have just begun your journey of faith in Christ or you have been a child of His for many years, God's desire is to transform your life to make you more and more like Christ. First John 1:9 says: *"If we confess our sins, He is faithful and righteous to forgive us our sins and to cleanse us from all unrighteousness."*

   To continue growing more like Christ, take a moment now and confess all known sin to God, including all thoughts that displease the Lord—especially any areas of pride.

2. First John 5:11–13 assures us of our position in God's Kingdom. Write down the promises you find in these verses for your own life.

3. Write out a short prayer of thanks to God for His incredible love and forgiveness toward you.

Allowing God to Transform Me

First John 5:11–13 is a critical verse for our foundation in Christ. When difficult times come, we can begin to doubt God's presence in our life. Therefore, repeat this verse frequently each day. It will help you walk steadily with God regardless of your circumstances.

Lesson 2
"Practicing Transparent Repentance"

Reading: chapter 8.

Spending Time with God

When you received Christ as your Savior, you also received His complete forgiveness. But if you still have unconfessed sin in your life, you will feel cut off from His peace and presence. And as long as you refuse to confess your sin, your actions will not reflect Christ's life within you, nor will you experience His power to change. That's an incredibly miserable state for a believer!

Can you recall a time when you felt this way? Psalm 32:3,4 reveals how David felt about his sin. *"When I kept silent about my sin, my body wasted away through my groaning all day long. For day and night Your hand was heavy upon me; my vitality was drained away as with the fever heat of summer."* Express to God your feelings about what sin has caused in your life.

Evaluating My Views

1. What is your perspective about Satan's goals for your life?

2. In what ways do you "toy" with sin and temptations?

3. Take the following "spiritual angiogram." Answer these questions about your heart attitude:

---

1. Is my heart broken and tender before the Lord?
2. Am I ready to be used for God's purposes at a moment's notice?
3. Is there any sin in my life that I have not yet confessed to God?
4. Am I practicing transparent repentance as soon as the Holy Spirit convicts me of sin?

Finding God's Perspective

1. Read John 10:10. Describe the long-term effects on your life of giving in to the enemy's temptations. Then describe the effects of following Christ.

2. God compares His work of removing sin and impurities from our lives with the purifying process of refining silver. According to Proverbs 25:4, what is the result of cleansing our lives of sin?

3. What attitude does God want us to have about this refining process (Hebrews 12:9–11)?

4. Using 1 John 1:9 and Ephesians 5:18 as a guide, describe the two steps in spiritual breathing.

Checking My Heart

One "little" sin can cost us everything! In 1 Samuel 10:1,8 and 13:7–14, we see an example in the life of King Saul. He didn't wait to offer sacrifices according to God's specific instructions—and it cost him his crown.

1. What excuses have you given for your actions when you disobeyed God's Word?

2. John the Baptist said, *"Therefore bring forth fruit in keeping with repentance"* (Matthew 3:8). What "fruits of repentance" need to happen in your own life now?

3. What acts of transparent repentance will you do to bring that about?

Allowing God to Transform Me

We need to remember what sin will cause in our life. Over the next week, look up the verses below and reflect on the destruction sin causes and on the peace and joy that obedience brings. Practice transparent repentance the moment you sense God's conviction.

SIN[1]	
• Steals joy (Ps.51:12)	• Opens the door to other sins (Is.30:1)
• Removes confidence (1 Jn.3:19–21)	• Causes frustration (Job 5:2)
• Brings guilt (Ps.51:3)	• Breaks fellowship (Is.59:1,2)
• Hinders usefulness for the Lord (1 Cor.3:1-3)	• Produces fear (Ps.34:4)
• Gives Satan the upper hand (2 Cor.2:9–11)	• Feeds the flesh (Rom.6)
• Quenches God's Spirit (1 Thes.5:18,19)	• Clouds eternal value system (Col.3:1,2)
• Brings physical damage (Ps.38:1–11; 31:10)	• Affects others (Gal.5:9)
• Causes ache in my bones (Ps.32:3,4)	• Brings disgrace on the name of the Lord (Rom.2:24)
• Destroys boldness (Prov.28:1)	• Makes me its slave (Jn.8:34, Gal.4:9)
• Breaks God's heart (Ps.78:41)	• *"Whatever is not from faith is sin"* (Rom.14:23)

Lesson 3
"Clear Conscience;
Conviction vs. Condemnation"

Reading: In chapter 8, review the sections titled "Restoring Relationships with Others" and "Conviction vs. Condemnation."

Spending Time with God

An impure heart cuts us off from experiencing God's presence. But through transparent repentance, we are made to be clean vessels again, usable for His perfect purposes. Psalm 51:10 says, *"Create in me a clean heart, O God, and renew a steadfast spirit within me."* Ask the Lord to continue purifying your life and to make you open to areas He may desire to uncover. Thank Him that everything He does in your life is done out of love.

Evaluating My Views

1. How do you think it would feel to have made things right with everyone in your life as much as you are able?

2. What are some failures in your past that seem to hinder your spiritual growth now?

3. Why do you think condemnation is such an effective tool of the enemy's?

Finding God's Perspective

1. Read Matthew 5:24 and Romans 12:18. What is God's attitude toward our relationship with others?

2. According to Hebrews 10:14, what is our standing as believers before God?

3. Describe what God wants our attitude to be as we maintain transparent repentance and a clear conscience (Hebrews 10:22,23).

Checking My Heart

"Having a clear conscience means that there is no one alive that I have ever wronged, offended, or hurt in any way that I have not gone back to and sought to make it right with both God and the individual."[2]

1. To have unhindered fellowship with God by establishing a clear conscience, of whom do you need to seek forgiveness? (Start with the hardest ones first.)

2. Do you understand the difference between God's conviction and Satan's condemnation? Are there areas in your life where Satan is defeating you through his relentless condemnation? In each space within the "Condemnation" side of the chart, describe a situation in which you are battling Satan's condemnation. Then fill in the side under "Conviction" as to how *God* wants you to deal with this particular issue.

Conviction	Condemnation
What is God's conviction concerning this issue?	What condemnation am I battling that comes from Satan?
How does God's conviction focus on a *specific* attitude or action regarding the issue I named? (Ex: "My impatience with my child was sin before God.")	How does Satan's condemnation focus *generally* on my character/who I am? (Ex: "I'm such a failure. I'm a terrible mother.")
What will happen when I confess this particular sin to God? (What changes will I see?)	What will likely happen in my particular situation if I continue listening to the enemy's condemnation? (Ex: further guilt, depression, defeat, poor self image.)
Action: When convicted, confess the specific sin to God (and others, if applicable), then claim His forgiveness. (1 John 1:9)	Action: When condemned, make sure you have confessed the specific sin to God (and others, if applicable), then claim the forgiveness of your sins and the righteousness of who you are in Christ. (Hebrews 10:14)

Allowing God to Transform Me

Oh, the blessed freedom that comes from knowing Christ, living in transparent repentance, and maintaining a clear conscience! Living in the freedom and forgiveness of Christ transforms our entire perspective on life, allowing us to demonstrate Christ's love to our husband, to our children, and to others. Praise God that *"He who began a good work in you will be faithful to complete it"* (Philippians 1:6).

Continue to practice transparent repentance by doing whatever is necessary to gain a clear conscience. Refuse Satan's condemnations and claim Hebrews 10:14.

Lesson 4
"I Don't Have to Choose Sin Anymore"

Reading: chapter 9

Spending Time with God

Consider how sin can become like a prison in a Christian's life. When you sin, you are taken captive by your lusts, selfishness, and pride. You are no longer free to live the victorious life in Christ that you want to live. And each time you sin, you are driven deeper into your prison. But God has flung open the prison doors! He has given us the power to live free of sin and to experience the peace of His forgiveness. Take a few moments to write a prayer of thanksgiving to God for the freedom we can experience through Christ.

Evaluating My Views

As you answer each of the following questions, develop a "before and after" picture of your spiritual journey. Examine your life before you were a Christian and after you took that step of faith in Christ. How has your life changed? (If you became a Christian as a child, compare your ideas as an immature Christian with your ideas as a more mature believer.)

1. What was different in your nature before your decision and after?
   Before:

   After:

2. Which sins were unbreakable habits before and what freedoms have you experienced after?
Before:

After:

3. What does the phrase, "As a Christian, I don't have to choose to sin anymore!" mean to you personally?

Finding God's Perspective

1. How does God say we should regard our sin (Colossians 3:3–10; Romans 6:6)?

2. According to 1 Corinthians 10:13, what temptations could prove too powerful to resist?

   Dr. Bill Bright says, "Because of Christ's sacrifice, we are as dead to sin as a corpse is dead to this world. It cannot respond to any pleasure the world offers. No appealing aroma, glitzy picture or sultry music can cause that dead body to get up and indulge. In the same way, we are to consider ourselves dead to the desires and attractions of sin."[3]

3. How can you practice being dead to sin (Galatians 5:16; Colossians 3:5)?

Checking My Heart

In *The Wycliffe Bible Commentary*, we read: "Flesh and Spirit are opposites, locked in continual combat. If the Christian is walking by the power of one, he cannot be in the control of the other."[4]

1. How do you tend to handle temptations?

2. Describe the process of how you can now victoriously respond to any and every temptation that you encounter. (Look at Chapter 9, the section titled "Living Inside Out.")

Allowing God to Transform Me

Our lives are like a ball on a hill. The ball is either being pushed up the road or is rolling back down, but it cannot sit stationary on a hill. Similarly, the road climbing toward God is challenging and difficult, while the road descending away from Him is easy and comfortable.

Obedience and the resulting holiness in our everyday life doesn't just happen accidentally. They require purposeful choices. If we're not pushing up the hill toward godliness by intentional planning, then we'll immediately roll back down toward spiritual dullness by becoming hardened and insensitive to the Lord. Without a constant yielding of our lives to the Spirit, our old fleshly habit patterns will gravitate toward sin every time.

This very day, you are establishing a pattern of either trust and dependence on the Lord to flee from temptation or a pattern of depending on your own flesh and giving into temptation at every turn. The decisions you make today do affect your future. *"Do not be deceived: God cannot be mocked. A man reaps what he sows. The one who sows to please his sinful nature, from that nature will reap destruction; the one who sows to please the Spirit, from the Spirit will reap eternal life. Let us not become weary in doing good, for at the proper time we will reap a harvest if we do not give up"* (Galatians 6:7–9, NIV).

Ask God to remind you moment by moment to call on the strength of His Spirit within you; then choose to respond in righteousness.

Lesson 5
"On the Altar"

Reading: In chapter 9, review the section titled "On The Altar" to the end of the chapter.

Spending Time with God

Living "inside out" describes the Spirit-controlled life, which is choosing the Spirit over the flesh moment by moment. An essential part of Spirit-controlled living is to focus on God through praise. Read Psalm 89:11–16. Using the thoughts in this passage, tell God how wonderful and wise He is.

Evaluating My Views

1. Are you practicing living from the inside out, calling on the power of the Spirit and choosing righteousness? What changes have you noticed in your life as a result?

2. What are some areas of your life that have yet to be yielded to the Lord's full control (thoughts, attitudes, responses, actions)?

3. What keeps you from consistently yielding these areas to the Lord?

4. Why do you think dying to self is so hard?

Finding God's Perspective

The opposite of pride is humility. Humility is seeing myself through the eyes of the Lord. Humility is realizing how self-centered I am and how desperately I need God and His work in my life. The insightful Christian writer C.S.

Lewis said, "If anyone would like to acquire humility, I can, I think, tell him the first step. The first step is to realize that one is proud. And a biggish step, too. At least, nothing whatever can be done before it. If you think you are not conceited, it means you are very conceited indeed."[5]

1. What is God's attitude toward pride and humility (James 4:6)?

2. Read John 15:4,5. What does Jesus tell us is the result of trying to live in our own strength?

3. Recognizing our pride and our desperate need for Christ's work within us, how can we surrender to the Lord each day (Romans 6:13; 12:1)?

4. What does Psalm 145:9,17 tell us about being able to trust the Lord's will for our life?

Checking My Heart

I (Judy) often picture myself as a lump of clay on the altar, willing to be molded and shaped and used for whatever the Lord chooses (Isaiah 64:8). At first, it was frightening to be so vulnerable. But God's love toward us is so great! He promises that nothing can ever separate us from His love (Romans 8:38,39), and He gives us only that which is for our good (Romans 8:28). He made us, so He alone knows what is the very best for each of us. Therefore, *our* job is to stay on the altar, a living sacrifice for the Lord to work through. *God's* job is to transform us.

1. What do you need to do when you find yourself in control again and have crawled (or leaped) off His altar? (Refer to "On The Altar," chapter 9.)

2. Although we are emotional creatures, God's Word is always truer than anything we may feel. How do your daily choices illustrate this truth?

Allowing God to Transform Me

Paul wrote in Galatians 2:20, *"I have been crucified with Christ; and it is no longer I who live, but Christ lives in me; and the life which I now live in the flesh I live by faith in the Son of God, who loved me and gave Himself up for me."*

The Spirit-controlled life is a process that requires the moment-by-moment practice of yielding our life to the Lord and choosing His power to respond rightly. As we practice crucifying our prideful, selfish flesh by laying our life on His altar each day, we *will* see growth and change. God is committed to making us more and more like Christ.

Daily yielding your life, however, does not mean that everything will suddenly be perfect. Your spiritual growth in some areas may be slow and difficult. And if you have experienced a breakdown in your marital relationship because of your sinful choices or neglect, the rebuilding process may be difficult. *But don't get discouraged!* God is faithful! As you begin to practice dying on the altar daily, you *will* witness His transforming work in your life.

Start now by picturing yourself on an altar before the Lord. Make a commitment that you will give Him all that you are, and all that you will be—rich or poor, sick or well, dead or alive. As you practice this each day, you will be *amazed* at the effect on your entire life, your marriage, your children, and your relationships with all who love you!

Note: If you will *not* be meeting with a discussion group or with another person to go through the Discussion Guide, please turn now to page 124 and go through the questions and new material for Week Three as if it were another daily lesson. You won't want to miss the additional insights found there!

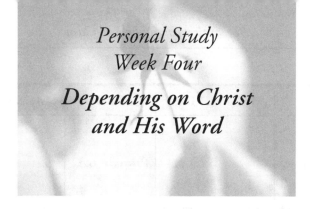

Depending on Christ and His Word

Lesson 1
"Our Desperate Need"

Reading: chapter 10

Spending Time with God

What we believe about God determines our entire worldview. That, in turn, affects everything we think and do. Bible teacher and writer Warren Wiersbe says, "When your theology is wrong, everything else follows."[1] Therefore, seeking to know God and His ways is worth far more than any other endeavor. He tells us to *"seek first His kingdom and His righteousness"* (Matthew 6:33).

As you read Jeremiah 9:23,24, ask God to give you an understanding of your desperate need to know Him: *"Thus says the Lord, 'Let not a wise man boast of his wisdom, and let not the mighty man boast of his might, let not a rich man boast of his riches; but let him who boasts boast of this, that he understands and knows Me, that I am the Lord who exercises lovingkindness, justice and righteousness on earth; for I delight in these things,' declares the Lord."*

Evaluating My Views

Our new lifestyle "in Christ" is completely different from our old life in our natural flesh (Galatians 5:17). Therefore, we constantly need to know God's perspective on every part of life. Compare what you thought about each of the following topics before you started this study with what God's Word says and your views now.

Subject	My Former Ideas	God's Word	My New Views
The consequences of adultery		Proverbs 6:32	
Having lustful thoughts toward another man		Matthew 5:27,28	
Pride		Proverbs 29:23	
My "human nature" apart from Christ		Psalm 16:2	

Finding God's Perspective

Paul reminds us that our old fleshly nature is completely corrupt when he says, *"For I know that nothing good dwells in me, that is, in my flesh"* (Romans 7:18).

1. According to Romans 12:1,2, what should our response be to this dilemma?

2. Why do we need to spend so much time with God (Isaiah 55:8,9)?

3. What is the result of not spending time with God and therefore cutting off the flow of Christ's power and transforming work (John 15:4,5)?

Checking My Heart

God tells us that *"as in water face reflects face, so the heart of man reflects man"* (Proverbs 27:19). Just like we see the reflection of our face in the water, so our heart reflects what we really are inside. A changed heart = changed actions. Take this "heart check" by honestly answering "yes" or "no" to each question.

Circle your answers:

1. Do I believe in my heart that apart from Christ's life in me, I am totally fallen and *"have no good thing"* (Psalm 16:2)?

YES   NO

2. Do I believe in my heart that without Christ working through me, I am capable of any sin, and I can do nothing that is truly good or of eternal value (John 15:4,5)?

YES   NO

Reflect on your answers. Were there any "no" answers? Were there any less-than-confident "yes" answers? When we come to truly see our fallen nature, we will confront our desperate need to be transformed by the Lord each day.

Allowing God to Transform Me

Begin every prayer time this week with Psalm 16:2 and John 15:5: *"I said to the Lord, 'You are my Lord; apart from you I have no good thing'"* (NIV). *"He who abides in Me, and I in him, he bears much fruit; for apart from Me you can do nothing."* Ask the Lord to inscribe these truths onto your heart and to show you your desperate need for His presence and His work in your life each day.

Also ask Him to show you what you are like apart from His transforming work. You will be appalled at what spews forth from your life! It will bring you to a very real understanding of your desperate need for His work in your life *every day.*

Lesson 2
"Daily Dependence on God Transforms Our Lives"

Reading: review chapter 10.

Spending Time with God

As we grow in knowing God, it is critically important that we develop a *biblical* view of who He is. We do this by studying His Word. It is also vitally important to be involved in a Bible-believing local church that helps guide us into a correct, biblical knowledge of God. As you read 1 Chronicles 29:10–13, ask God to help you grow in understanding His ways.

"So David blessed the Lord in the sight of all the assembly; and David said, 'Blessed are You, O Lord God of Israel our father, forever and ever. Yours, O Lord, is the greatness and the power and the glory and the victory and the majesty, indeed everything that is in the heavens and the earth; Yours is the dominion, O Lord, and You exalt Yourself as head over all. Both riches and honor come from You, and You rule over all, and in Your hand is power and might; and it lies in Your hand to make great and to strengthen everyone. Now therefore, our God, we thank You, and praise Your glorious name.'"

Evaluating My Views

Is your Christian walk consistent or inconsistent? Are you depending on God or on your own efforts? Think about the following areas of your relationship with your husband and with others. Which of these areas are most difficult for you in demonstrating a consistent spiritual life? Mark one or more.

❑ Temper outbursts/ patience

❑ Lust/ pure thoughts

❑ Selfishness/ selflessness

❑ Sharp tongue/ words of edification

❑ Holding grudges/ forgiving

❑ Self-dependent/ relying on God

❑ Irritable spirit/ Spirit-controlled

❑ Critical spirit/ accepting

❑ Proud/ humble

❑ **Want to be served/ demonstrating servanthood**

❑ Deceit/ honesty

Finding God's Perspective

Because of our fallen flesh, we can never be spiritually consistent on our own. That's why we must yield our lives to the Lord each day, depending on His transforming work through us. Only then can we be available and ready for God to use at a moment's notice. For example, in the Old Testament book of Esther, a regular Jewish girl finds herself catapulted into the role of queen. More than that, she then faces a life-or-death decision of whether to step forward and reveal her Jewish nationality to try and save her people, or to remain quiet. Esther *did* step forward, and in so doing, saved the Jews from slaughter. That was her moment.

1. What did Esther's uncle, Mordecai, say to her in Esther 4:14?

2. What does God tell us can happen if we don't keep our heart tender to the Lord each day (Hebrews 3:12,13)?

3. What happens in our lives as we die daily and allow Christ's Spirit to transform us (Galatians 5:22,23)?

We never know when God may choose to use us. And if we are out of fellowship with Him, we may miss an incredible opportunity. It won't change *God's* plans. He will always accomplish His will regardless—but I don't want to miss out on being His special instrument!

Checking My Heart

Apart from Christ, we can do nothing of eternal value. With Christ living through us, we can do all He asks of us. If we remain dependent on the Lord, He can use us at a moment's notice. Yet we are so weak!

1. How does God tell us to view our weaknesses in 2 Corinthians 12:9,10?

God will *"equip you in every good thing to do His will, working in us that which is pleasing in His sight, through Jesus Christ"* (Hebrews 13:21) if you will just lay your life on His altar and let Him work!

We've looked at pride and humility. Pride says, "I can do pretty well today without yielding myself in absolute dependence on Christ's help." Humility realizes my weaknesses and that I have no means within myself with which to bring forth any righteousness, any goodness, any kindness. Without time in His presence, my perspective will be skewed, my words will be fleshly, and my attitude will be selfish.

2. What is my perspective each morning on how I will get through the day?

3. What do my daily choices reveal about my dependence on the Lord?

4. What differences can people recognize in my life that point to consistent time spent with the Creator?

Allowing God to Transform Me

Continue to ask God to implant in your heart the conviction that apart from Christ's Spirit, you have "no good thing," and that apart from Christ's work through you, you can do nothing of eternal value. Continue praying Psalm 16:2 and John 15:5, and review the verses in the box toward the end of Chapter 10 until this truth drives you to desperate, daily dependence on the Lord.

Lesson 3
"The Effect of God's Word in Our Lives"

Reading: chapter 11

Spending Time with God

Psalm 119 emphasizes the importance of God's Word. Write down your thoughts under each verse about why it is so important for us to know His Word:

119:98–100 –"Your commandments make me wiser than my enemies, for they are ever mine. I have more insight than all my teachers, for Your testimonies are my meditation. I understand more than the aged, because I have observed Your precepts."

119:105 – "Your word is a lamp to my feet and a light to my path."

119:165 – "Those who love Your law have great peace, and nothing causes them to stumble."

Listening to God as He speaks to us through the Bible allows us to know Him and to grow more like Christ. Thank the Lord for giving us His precious Word.

Evaluating My Views

Many Christians believe the Bible and believe that it is important, yet they don't make the effort to know it well. Take this little quiz about the Bible. See how familiar you are with God's Book.

1. How many books does the Bible contain?
2. Which book in the Bible has the creation account?
3. Which book tells the history of the early church?
4. Name the person who wrote the greatest number of books in the New Testament.

How did you do? (Check your answers with those at the end of this lesson.) However, far more important than knowing *about* the Bible is knowing the *author* of the Bible—God. That is our goal for digging into God's Word.

Finding God's Perspective

1. What does God tell us about being able to trust His Word even when life's circumstances seem contradictory (Psalm 119:160; Proverbs 19:21)?

2. What should our response be to God's Word (1 Thessalonians 2:13)?

3. In Psalm 19:7–11, we see changes that the Word can produce in our lives. What are some of them?

Checking My Heart

1. What kinds of situations make me doubt or question God's Word?

2. What thoughts do I frequently nurture that are not in line with God's truth?

3. What choices and actions do I find myself making that are not based on God's Word?

Allowing God to Transform Me

What kinds of answers did you give for "Checking My Heart"? Can you say with the psalmist, *"I esteem right all Your precepts concerning everything, I hate every false way"* (Psalm 119:128)? Allow God to change these areas so that they conform to His Word. Pray about each area now, asking God to transform your heart through the power of the Holy Spirit. Search God's Word for His wisdom on difficult-to-understand areas. If needed, practice transparent repentance.

(Answers to questions: 1. 66, 2. Genesis, 3. Acts, 4. The Apostle Paul)

Lesson 4
"Establishing Daily Time with God"

Reading: Review chapter 11 from the section titled "What To Study" to the end of the chapter.

Spending Time with God

Ask God to give you a deep desire to study, read, and apply His Word to your life. *"As the deer pants for the water brooks, so my soul pants for You, O God"* (Psalm 42:1).

Evaluating My Views

We are going to discuss how to study God's Word. To prepare yourself, write your answers to these questions:

• What are you curious about or interested to learn about in God's Word?

• Is there a topic of which you would like to know God's perspective? What is it?

• Which Bible character fascinates you?

• What attributes or aspects of God's character seem unclear to you?

Finding God's Perspective

1. According to Hebrews 4:12, what does the Bible do in our lives?

Andrew Murray writes: "There may be a study and knowledge of the Word, in which there is but little real fellowship with the living God. But there is also a reading of the Word, in the very presence of the Father, and under the leading of the Spirit, in which the Word comes to us in living power from God Himself; it is to us the very voice of the Father, a real personal blessing and strength, and awakens the response of a living faith that reaches the heart of God again."[2]

2. What does this quote say about our Quiet Times with God?

3. What should we do to enter into the presence of the living God (Matthew 6:6; Psalm 131:2)?

Checking My Heart

One thing is absolutely 100 percent guaranteed—time with the Lord won't "just happen." If you wait until you are motivated and it seems easy to spend time with Him, you'll find yourself one day standing before His throne without ever having gotten to know Him! Time in God's presence truly is the most important thing you will do each day. To help you start spending daily time with God, fill out this Quiet Time chart:

I am going to meet with God at _____each day.
place

The time I will spend with Him is from _____ to _____

I will study this topic/ issue/ book of the Bible: _____

To make this Quiet Time a reality, I need to: _____

Allowing God to Transform Me

Ask God to continue implanting in your heart the reason why it is so utterly critical for you to cling to Him each day in order to be renewed and transformed through His Word and His presence. As you spend time in His presence, begin recording what God impresses on your mind during your daily Quiet Time.

Lesson 5
"Dying, Adoring, Confessing, and Arming"

Reading: chapter 12.

Spending Time with God

Christ taught us to recognize and praise God for His virtues: *"Our Father who is in heaven, hallowed be Your name"* (Matthew 6:9). In His Name resides all that He is. Read these psalms and spend a few moments praising God right now for His holy name. He is worthy of all our praise!

> Psalm 148:13 - *"Let them praise the name of the Lord, for His name alone is exalted; His glory is above earth and heaven."*

> Psalm 99:3 - *"Let them praise Your great and awesome name; holy is He."*

Evaluating My Views

God tells us that when we cover ourselves with His armor each day, we will be able to stand firm in every battle (Ephesians 6:13). Describe how donning each piece of God's armor can affect your entire day. (Refer back to "The Armor of God" section in the book if needed.)

1. Girding your loins with truth:

2. Putting on the breastplate of righteousness:

3. Shodding your feet with the gospel of peace:

4. Taking up the shield of faith:

5. Putting on the helmet of salvation:

6. Taking up the sword of the Spirit:

Finding God's Perspective

Christ lived with more demands on Him and more people seeking His attention than we will ever experience. Everywhere He went, hundreds of people crowded Him just to touch His garment or to ask Him questions. *"But He Himself would often slip away to the wilderness and pray"* (Luke 5:16). If God on earth frequently needed a quiet, lonely place in which to pray, how much more do you and I!

But to be honest, almost every day I (Judy) face a battle when it comes time to pray. As an active person, I struggle to sit still. However, that isn't the real battle. The *real* war is against my pride. Prayer humbles my soul to seek and depend on God, thus crucifying pride. And my pride doesn't *like* to be crucified!

1. Read Luke 18:9–14, and describe the prayer attitude God desires.

2. In Luke 6:12–16 we see Jesus' example of prayer just before an important time in His ministry. Read these verses and describe what Jesus did.

3. God loves for us to pray specifically. He provides many examples throughout Scripture of His specific answers to specific prayers. King David asked the Lord specific questions when he was being attacked by the Philistines. Read 2 Samuel 5:17–25. How can this be an example for your prayers?

4. How can unconfessed sin affect your prayer life (Psalm 66:18; Isaiah 59:1,2)?

Checking My Heart

Ask yourself these questions about your prayer life:

- Is pride and self-dependence keeping me from meeting humbly with God in prayer?

- Am I practicing daily (hourly) laying my life on the altar for God to do with as He chooses?

- Do I find adoration toward the Lord to be easy or difficult? Would knowing more about His attributes help me praise Him more fully?

- Is there any sin that has begun to fester and decay in my life? What keeps me from confessing that now?

Now ask yourself: Will I practice putting on each piece of God's armor this week to protect and prepare every part of my life against the devil's schemes?

Allowing God to Transform Me

The following Quiet Time model can be adapted for your own use. As you have your Quiet Time according to your schedule from the previous lesson, begin practicing the four steps of Dying, Adoring, Confessing, and Arming. Practice putting on each piece of God's armor, and keep His armor in mind throughout the day to remind you to flee from sin and to resist the enemy.

Note: If you will *not* be meeting with a discussion group or with another person to go through the Discussion Guide, please turn now to page 127 and go through the questions and new material for Week Four as if it were another daily lesson. You won't want to miss the additional insights found there!

Quiet Time Model

Go to your quiet place where you can focus on the Lord.

Open in prayer:

Ask God to meet with you, and ask Him to give you His insight into His Word. *"Open my eyes, that I may behold wonderful things from Your law"* (Psalm 119:18).

Time in the Bible:

As you do your Bible study, write down on a piece of paper everything that ministers, convicts, or speaks to your heart. (If you sense God's conviction, practice transparent repentance right then so that your fellowship with Him will remain unhindered.)

Time in Prayer:

Dying: Lay your life on the altar before God: "Rich or poor, sick or well, dead or alive, I am completely Yours, Lord, to do with whatever You choose."

Adoration: Praise Him for His marvelous attributes, such as His grace, His love, His faithfulness, His wisdom, His power, His majesty, etc.

Confession: Ask God to search your heart, praying Psalm 139:23,24: *"Search me, O God, and know my heart; try me and know my anxious thoughts; and see if there be any hurtful way in me, and lead me in the everlasting way."* Immediately confess anything He may show you.

Arming: Put on each piece of His armor *"so that you will be able to stand firm against the schemes of the devil"* (Ephesians 6:11):

> *Gird your loins with truth:* Pray: "Lord, I gird my loins with Your truth. Please weave Your Word into my life as part of the fabric of my being." Then ask God to apply in your life the things that He showed you from your Bible study time. Pray through the things that you wrote down. Also review any verse you are committing to memory at this time.
>
> ***Put on the breastplate of righteousness:*** Pray: "Lord Jesus, I put You on as my breastplate of righteousness because I have no good besides You, and I can do nothing of eternal value apart from You" (Psalm 16:2,

John 15:5). Picture "putting on" Christ, and ask Him to speak with your lips, think with your mind, and see through your eyes that entire day, in every circumstance.

Shod your feet with the gospel of peace: Pray: "Lord, I shod my feet with the preparation of the gospel of peace in order to flee from evil and to run to You for Your strength and protection." Picture fleeing from any situation that you know is not honoring to the Lord.

Take up the shield of faith: Pray: "Lord, I take up the shield of faith." Then pray "by faith" for the prayer requests on your heart, demonstrating your complete dependence on His answers. Trust that His will is perfect and good, carried out in complete love.

Take the helmet of salvation: Pray: "Lord, I put on the helmet of salvation." Then picture His helmet covering your eyes, ears, and mind to keep you from seeing, hearing, or thinking anything that displeases Him.

Take up the sword of the Spirit: Pray: "Lord, I take up the sword of the Spirit and ask that You will remind me to resist Satan according to Your Word throughout this day." Then when a temptation or condemnation comes along, say aloud, "Satan, I resist you in the name of the Lord Jesus Christ" according to James 4:7.

End your prayer time by thanking God for the work He is doing in your life and in those around you—especially your husband and your family. Then rise up *"in the strength of His might"* (Ephesians 6:10)!

Personal Study
Week Five

*Demonstrating Holiness
in Every Area*

Lesson 1
"Elements of Obedience"

Reading: chapter 13.

Spending Time with God

God tells us that when Christ's Spirit lives within us, we not only have the power to obey, but we also have the desire to obey: *"For it is God who works in you **to will** and **to act** according to his good purpose"* (Philippians 2:13, NIV, emphasis added). Thank the Lord that He gives us the desire and the ability to walk in righteousness. What a gift He has given us!

Evaluating My Views

Look at the contrast between obedience and disobedience found in these verses:

Obedience: *"I considered my ways and turned my feet to Your testimonies. I hastened and did not delay to keep Your commandments"* (Psalm 119:59,60).

Disobedience: *"Why do you call Me, 'Lord, Lord,' and do not do what I say?"* (Luke 6:46).

Which one do you think best describes your daily choices? List some specific choices that illustrate this.

Finding God's Perspective

The Bible shows us many examples of the results of obedience and disobedience. Contrast Joshua and Saul, two leaders of ancient Israel. How are they different in their approaches to obedience? Write your answers in the chart:

	Joshua	Saul
The beginning of his ministry for God	Numbers 27:15–23	1 Samuel 9:1,2; 10:1,9,10
His actions	Joshua 11:15	1 Samuel 15:10,11
His final days	Joshua 23:1–3; 24:29–31	1 Samuel 28:5,6,17–19; 31:2–6

Checking My Heart

Obedience is our responsibility—the outcome is *God's* responsibility. God measures our success or failure 100 percent by our obedience to Him. When God directs us to do something, we are to obey regardless of the results. The world, and even many Christians, may not always understand. But as the apostles said, *"We must obey God rather than men"* (Acts 5:29). God deems those a success who totally obey *His* voice.

Fill in the three elements of obedience mentioned in chapter 13:

> 1. Obedience is a _____, never based on my feelings.
>
> 2. Obedience is _____, because delay leads me into ever-increasing sin.
>
> 3. Obedience is _____, following God's *entire* Word.

Which of these three seems the hardest for you? Why?

We always marvel at how some pastor or dynamic spiritual leader can end up in adultery. But "big" sins always start with one "little" choice of hardening our heart toward something the Lord has said. And that little choice makes the next choice of disobedience twice as easy. From there, it's a greased slide down the slope. And we are *all* one choice away from beginning that slide.

What do you need to do to stay off that slide?

Allowing God to Transform Me

Obedience to God's Word always leads me into righteousness. Each morning as I gird my loins with God's truth, I'm really saying, *"I choose to live by 'every word that proceeds out of the mouth of God'"* (Matthew 4:4). He says to flee sexual temptation, so I choose to avoid all enticing situations. He says to love the person who treats me poorly, so I choose to demonstrate His love regardless of feelings.

But walking in obedience requires a conscious effort. Write down three difficult areas in which you will obey God and His Word by the power of His Spirit this week. Remember to call on His power to obey moment by moment.

Lesson 2
"Motivations Behind Our Obedience"

Reading: Review chapter 13 from "Motivations for Obedience" to the end.

Spending Time with God

The Bible tells us that *"we love, because He first loved us"* (1 John 4:19). Christ says that our obedience demonstrates our love for the Lord. *"He who has My commandments and keeps them is the one who loves Me"* (John 14:21). Our love for God motivates us to obey Him. Meditate on this thought, then write a short love letter to God.

Evaluating My Views

If we fail to comprehend God's love and the enormity of Christ's sacrifice for us, then in turn we will lack love for Him. When that happens, we can fall into legalism. Legalism attempts to earn God's love by performing. But we don't need to "earn" His love—we already have it in fullest measure! However, it's easy for us to edge away from love into legalism. What may begin as a labor of love for God can turn into a set of rules. Rate yourself in the following areas of service to God. Draw a mark on the line where you think you are in the continuum. Then as you go through the lesson, keep these legalistic areas in mind so that you can surrender them once again to the Lord for *His* work through you.

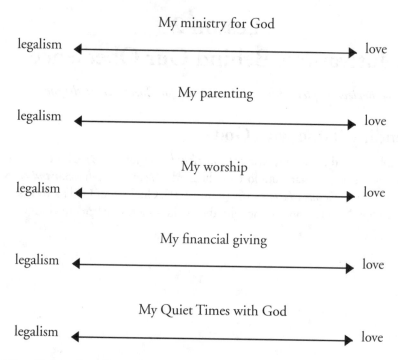

My ministry for God

legalism ←————————————————————→ love

My parenting

legalism ←————————————————————→ love

My worship

legalism ←————————————————————→ love

My financial giving

legalism ←————————————————————→ love

My Quiet Times with God

legalism ←————————————————————→ love

Finding God's Perspective

When we find ourselves trying to earn God's love or favor, we need to repent of self-righteous efforts that count for nothing (John 15:5) and yield our life back to the One who works His righteousness through us. Legalism and disobedience both are corrected by having proper motivations for obeying and serving God.

1. What does Psalm 25:10 say about obedience motivated by trust?

2. Proverbs 1:32,33 gives us a contrast between disobedience and obedience. How do these verses encourage us to obey for our own protection?

3. What can we learn from Abraham and Moses about being motivated to obey because of our future rewards (Hebrews 11:8–10,24–26)?

4. Contrast the situations that brought Paul joy and sorrow in Philemon 7 and 2 Timothy 4:14. What does this tell us about our obedience or disobedience and its effects on others?

Checking My Heart

Let's take another "spiritual angiogram" concerning obedience:

- Have you predetermined to obey whatever God shows you each day?
- Do you see in your life a pattern of responding to God's conviction with immediate obedience, or do you tend to delay, demonstrating *dis*obedience?
- Have you determined to obey *all* of God's Word, even if it seems hard, inconvenient, or downright painful to do so?
- Do you find motivation to obey the Lord because you trust Him and understand that obedience protects you from consequences you can't possibly see?
- Do you find it motivating to obey because God promises blessings and rewards to those who keep His statutes?
- Do you believe that *no act of disobedience is insignificant*? Consequently, do you understand how hardness in your heart affects your choices and your actions, thereby affecting everyone around you?

Allowing God to Transform Me

We've spent a good deal of time talking about living the Spirit-controlled life and having daily time with the Lord. Why? Because these are *the two most essential elements* in any faithful believer's life. One without the other leads to sin, whether that is infidelity or any other act of disobedience. Ask God to continue developing in you an understanding of your desperate need for His Word and His work in and through you each day. As you "put on Christ" each day, ask Him to remind you to obey instantly and completely, drawing on His power to do so. You will be amazed at the results!

Lesson 3
"Confronting Integrity"

Reading: chapter 14.

Spending Time with God

Whatever we focus on determines what we will become. If our eyes remain on the Lord, He fills our mind with His truth and we become more and more like Christ. But if we fill our minds with romantic soap operas, sensual music, and trash from the Internet, our minds become like a garbage landfill.

As believers, we are actually God's temple! Therefore, God's Word calls us to holiness. Read and ponder 2 Corinthians 6:16–7:1. Make greater purity and integrity a focus for this study.

Evaluating My Views

Just as Christ chastised the Pharisees for washing the outside of the cup while leaving it full of filth on the inside (Luke 11:39), we need to deliberately scrutinize all that we do, both privately and publicly, examining each choice to make sure it lines up with God's Word.

List the influences and choices in your life that are poor examples of integrity. These may be influences such as certain types of movies, books, magazines, and music that encourage impure thoughts or unbiblical behavior. Or you may write down activities such as work-related interactions that draw you toward another man. Perhaps you may list a friend who influences you to make wrong choices.

Finding God's Perspective

God convicted a policeman about a lie he told during work. Though he knew the consequences could be severe, he decided it was more important to have a clear conscience before the Lord and to restore his integrity than to cover the lie. So he revealed the truth to his boss—and lost his job. Did he regret that decision? He said later that restoring a clear conscience and regaining his integrity had given him such freedom and peace that he knew he had made the right decision. Even if maintaining integrity means losing the riches of this world, we must choose to live for the eternal.

1. According to 1 Peter 1:14–16, what should our standard be?

2. What does 1 John 2:15,16 tell us about loving the things of this world?

The Lord rewards integrity with gifts that last eternally and exceed *anything* we could have gained in this life. So although integrity may be costly for the moment, it is worth everything.

3. What kind of perspective on life and integrity does Psalm 103:15–18 give?

4. Living a life of integrity really begins where (Matthew 16:24)?

Checking My Heart

1. Jesus says in Luke 16:10, *"He who is faithful in a very little thing is faithful also in much; and he who is unrighteous in a very little thing is unrighteous also in much."* Describe what this passage reveals about your life and what you need to change.

2. Think of a situation you face right now that is testing your integrity. What are the choices you have?

3. How can you maintain your integrity even if it costs you something?

Allowing God to Transform Me

Follow through with your choices of integrity in the questions above. First, ask God to help you choose wisely. Then determine ways you can maintain your integrity. Also use your list under "Evaluating My Views" to help remind you of places where you need to be vigilant with your integrity, starting now.

Lesson 4
"Practicing Integrity"

Reading: Review chapter 14.

Spending Time with God

Living a life of integrity does not mean retreating into a cave and removing ourselves from the world's influence. Christ clearly tells us to be light *in* a darkened world. We must live among nonbelievers in such a way that our lives point them to Christ. On the other hand, we must keep ourselves from becoming entangled in the world's philosophies and sinful activities. Read the verses below and ask God to help you live in such a way that others see Christ in you.

"Let your light shine before men in such a way that they may see your good works, and glorify your Father who is in heaven" (Matthew 5:16).

"Dear friends, I urge you, as aliens and strangers in the world, to abstain from sinful desires, which war against your soul. Live such good lives among the pagans that, though they accuse you of doing wrong, they may see your good deeds and glorify God on the day he visits us" (1 Peter 2:11,12 NIV).

Evaluating My Views

Answer this integrity checklist, writing yes or no at the end of each question:

1. Does my behavior change when no one is looking or no one knows?

2. Do I swear under my breath?

3. Do I exaggerate or lie in "little" areas (like my weight)?

4. Do I think speeding to get my children to school on time is more important than modeling integrity before them?

5. Do I daydream about things God considers impure?

6. Do my shelves contain books, movies, magazines, CDs, or games that denigrate God's holy name?

7. Does my home contain "decorations" that are actually items of pagan worship?

How did you do? Did you answer any of these with a "yes"? Focus on these areas as you complete the day's study.

Finding God's Perspective

1. What instructions do you find in Psalm 51:6?

2. Which area of integrity does Proverbs 8:7,8 describe, and how can you apply this Scripture?

3. What does God specifically instruct you to do in Titus 2:11–14?

4. What is the contrast found in 1 John 2:3–6?

Checking My Heart

Prayerfully read Psalm 119:1–5:
"How blessed are those whose way is blameless, who walk in the law of the Lord.
How blessed are those who observe His testimonies, who seek Him with all their heart.
They also do no unrighteousness; they walk in His ways.
You have ordained Your precepts, that we should keep them diligently.
Oh that my ways may be established to keep Your statutes!"

Now go back and look at your "yes" answers in the "Evaluating My Views" section. Write down specific actions you need to take to bring these areas in line with God's standard of holiness and integrity.

Allowing God to Transform Me

Take several minutes of silence, allowing God to search your heart for any practices that you have accepted as normal, but which are really sin. Write down anything He brings to mind and what you need to do to re-establish integrity. Ask Him to help you follow through in making righteous choices.

Lesson 5
"Integrity and the Media"

Reading: chapter 15

Spending Time with God

"I will walk within my house in the integrity of my heart. I will set no worthless thing before my eyes; I hate the work of those who fall away; it shall not fasten its grip on me. A perverse heart shall depart from me; I will know no evil" (Psalm 101:2–4).

Which area of the media has the greatest allure for you? television? movies? books? magazines? the Internet? Select one and use it throughout this lesson to help you develop habits of integrity. If several areas present a challenge for you, work through this lesson again, focusing on each of the other media areas that trouble you. To begin, ask God to help you break any impure habits you may have regarding your selected area.

Evaluating My Views

Concerning the media area that poses the greatest purity challenge to you:
1. How much time do you spend on it each week?

2. What kinds of impure thoughts and actions are encouraged by participation in unholy aspects of this media?

3. By allowing impurity from this media into your life, how has this made you less sensitive to God's Spirit?

Finding God's Perspective

1. What action does 1 Thessalonians 5:21,22 tell us to take?

2. What always remains one of our strongest forms of defense against temptation (Psalm 119:11; Proverbs 7:1,3)?

3. What else does God tell us is critical for keeping our lives and actions pure and holy (Proverbs 11:14; 12:15)?

Checking My Heart

Read Psalm 101:2–4 again. Then answer these questions to find your I.Q. (Integrity Quotient):

• Can I honestly say that every part of Psalm 101:2–4 is true for me and my home?

• Do I justify attending movies or watching TV shows that contain content God calls perverted and impure?

• Do I tend to believe that implanting such images in my mind will not harm my life or my spiritual sensitivity?

• Am I willing to take the "R-rated Challenge?"

• Am I willing to begin examining *everything* I set before my eyes according to God's standards and to get rid of my cable or satellite service, or even the TV itself, if God directs me to do so?

• Have I given into temptations to view pornography? If not, have I pre-established guards and filters to keep me from falling into the quicksand of pornography? If so, am I willing to confess that to God and to my husband?

Allowing God to Transform Me

Go to God in prayer, asking Him to show you ways to re-establish integrity and purity in the area(s) which He has revealed. This can range from turning off your TV and setting up accountability in these areas, to canceling your cable subscription and your Internet access.

Then every day as you shod your feet with the gospel of peace (Ephesians 6:15), picture fleeing from evil by turning off your TV or your computer whenever anything unholy comes before your eyes. It's worth whatever it takes to have a pure heart before the Lord!

Note: If you will *not* be meeting with a discussion group or with another person to go through the Discussion Guide, please turn now to page 130 and go through the questions and new material for Week Five as if it were another daily lesson. You won't want to miss the additional insights found there!

Personal Study
Week Six
Living Out Christ's Love and
Caring for Your Marriage

Lesson 1
"Love and Feelings"

Reading: chapter 16

Spending Time with God

We have seen how living the Spirit-controlled life, spending daily time with the Lord, and living with integrity make a dramatic difference in our lives. But do they affect our marriage? Yes, in *every* way! When we remain in a right relationship with God, then His work within us *will* affect our marriage. But in order to be rightly related to our Lord, and consequently to our husband, we must also understand God's unique perspective on love.

Meditate on these verses that show the Lord's incredible love, and thank God that we can love Him and others because He first loved us:

> John 3:16 – *"For God so loved the world that He gave his one and only Son, that whoever believes in him shall not perish but have eternal life"* (NIV).

> Romans 5:8 – *"But God demonstrates His own love toward us, in that while we were yet sinners, Christ died for us."*

> 1 John 3:1 – *"See how great a love the Father has bestowed on us, that we would be called children of God; and such we are."*

Evaluating My Views

The weddings of past generations emphasized godly love and commitment to your mate. The vows to "love and honor" were taken more seriously. The ceremony held an air of solemn importance. Today, the average marriage ceremony focuses on romantic love, the vows are often flippant, and the ceremony may be as frivolous as skydiving or being married underwater. Often people will say, "Aren't they a cute couple? They're so in love."

While it's wonderful that the bride and groom gaze at one another with starry-eyed rapture, the important issue is what *kind* of love their nuptials are based upon. Is their marriage founded merely upon a romantic infatuation soon to wither and fade, or are they committed to one another based on the unconditional love of 1 Corinthians 13, demonstrated through patience, kindness, humility, selflessness, and forgiveness?

1. What kind of views do your friends have about marriage and the marriage ceremony?

2. How have your views on marriage changed since beginning this study?

3. How has this change affected your marriage?

Finding God's Perspective

1. Read 1 Corinthians 13. How does God's definition of love differ from the views you mentioned in the questions above?

2. Why is pursuing emotional love in an attraction outside your marriage as foolish as trying to build a house on a sand dune (Matthew 7:24–27)?

3. How did Jesus demonstrate selfless love (Philippians 2:5–8)?

4. We are told to *"have this attitude [of selfless love] in yourselves which was also in Christ Jesus"* (Philippians 2:5). What practical ways can you demonstrate the Philippians 2:5–8 type of love in your marriage?

To regard my husband as more important than myself means that I *choose* to focus on meeting his needs above my own, just as Christ chose to give His life to meet my needs. This is not saying that my husband is better than I am. Instead, I'm recognizing my high calling to serve him just as Christ served us. *"Let all that you do be done in love"* (1 Corinthians 16:14).

Checking My Heart

1. Apply the Philippians 2:3 "gold standard" to *"do nothing from selfishness or empty conceit, but with humility of mind regard one another as more important than yourselves"* specifically to a conflict in your marriage.

2. Describe how your feelings have worked against your marriage at times.

3. Which feelings do you need to put under the Spirit's control?

Allowing God to Transform Me

Write a "bullet prayer" that you can shoot up to God whenever your feelings get out of line in your marriage relationship. This week, pray that prayer each time your feelings begin to overshadow the need to demonstrate godly, sacrificial love.

Lesson 2
"Godly Love Protects Your Marriage"

Reading: In chapter 16, review the four points under the section "Love and Protection."

Spending Time with God

Dr. Bill Bright says of his marriage:

> Vonette and I have had 53 wonderful years of marriage, but had we not been spiritually minded, had we not both sought the will of the Lord, it would have been a disaster. Vonette is a very strong-willed woman and I, too, am very strong-willed. Each of us naturally has tended to want our own way and do our own thing. But from even during our engagement period before the wedding ceremony, we determined that with the help of the Holy Spirit we would seek first the kingdom of God and we would each invite our Lord Jesus to direct our lives and our marriage . . . He is the one who has preserved us through the years and will continue to do so as we walk in the Spirit and invite His control of our thoughts, attitudes, actions, motives, desire, and words.[1]

Matthew 6:33 tells us to *"seek first His kingdom and His righteousness, and all these things will be added to you."* If you haven't done so yet today, lay your life on His altar, seeking Him first. Then ask Jesus to direct every aspect of your life, including your marriage.

Evaluating My Views

Think of a recent incident in your marriage when your husband and you strongly disagreed. Evaluate how you approached the disagreement by writing out the ways you accomplished or failed to apply the following four points in the conflict:

1. I denied my own selfish desires.

2. I forgave or asked for forgiveness quickly.

3. I took any negative thoughts captive before and after the disagreement.

4. I gave up my rights for the sake of our relationship.

Finding God's Perspective

1. What does Proverbs 12:4 say about our roles as wives?

2. What principle can you apply to your closest friend (your husband) that Jesus gave us in John 15:13?

3. How does Ephesians 4:32 apply to your marriage?

Checking My Heart

Answer these questions about your family relationships, and write what changes you need to make:

• Do I depend on my feelings in order to demonstrate love?

• Do I allow my thoughts to dwell on all my husband's irritating quirks, or do I take those thoughts captive?

- Do I refuse to ask forgiveness, or do my children hear me apologize frequently, asking and giving forgiveness to my husband and to them?

- Do I hang onto my rights, becoming angry when my husband doesn't do things "my way," or do I practice yielding those rights to God?

- Does my family see me running to Christ for His strength because I understand that the quality of every single relationship in my life is dependent upon my relationship with Him?

Allowing God to Transform Me

If God has uncovered an area revealing a lack of His godly love, please stop and take the steps below that are necessary to make that area right.

★ Confess deep-seated pride and selfishness in your life and how that affects your marriage and family.

★ Ask forgiveness of someone.

★ Confess having dwelt on your husband's faults instead of thanking God for his qualities.

★ Yield to God the rights to which you are tenaciously clinging.

Whatever God has shown you, purpose to make these areas right immediately so that you can once again experience His forgiveness and peace and demonstrate His sacrificial love.

Lesson 3
"Our Testimony of Love"

Reading: Review in chapter 16 the sections titled "A Testimony to our Children" and "A Testimony to the World."

Spending Time with God

Consider the kind of love the Lord has for us: "*He who did not spare His own Son, but delivered Him over for us all, how will He not also with Him freely give us all things?*" (Romans 8:32). The horrific death Jesus faced was not something He was forced to do. He chose this death for our sakes. Thank Him for what He was willing to do out of love for you.

Evaluating My Views

How much of an influence are you on your world? Jesus came and died so that He and His followers would influence the world for God's glory. One way His love is demonstrated to the world is through the actions of believers. Evaluate your testimony to the world in these two areas:

1. When my children (or other close family members) look at how I treat my husband, what kind of influence have I been? (List both the good influences and the bad.)

2. When my neighbors or coworkers look at my marriage relationship, what do they see? (List the good and bad of what they see.)

Finding God's Perspective

We cannot control what our spouse does, and God does not expect us to. Our job is not to "fix" our husbands. But God *does* require that we display His love in all that we do. In turn, His love will influence our husbands, children, and many other people around us.

1. What kind of marriage relationship should you be building so that the world can see Jesus in you (Proverbs 31:10–12; 1 Peter 3:3,4)?

2. What does God expect us to produce in our lives (Galatians 5:22,23)?

3. How will this benefit your children?

Checking My Heart

Children imitate what they see demonstrated at home. It's so easy to let our behavior slide at home because that's where we feel most comfortable. Evaluate the following areas to see what you are modeling that your children will imitate:

My speech:

What I view or read:

Where I go during my free time:

My attitude and words to my husband:

How I handle minor crises:

How I spend money:

Allowing God to Transform Me

Which one of the areas above is your weakest? Continually practice transparent repentance (confessing the sin, laying your life back on the altar, and giving Christ full control again) as you deal with this area and other areas that the Lord may reveal this week. As we live the Spirit-controlled life and demonstrate godly love toward our spouse, our marriage will shine as a beacon to a searching world.

Lesson 4
"The Priority of Your Marriage"

Reading: chapter 17.

Spending Time with God

Take a prayer tour of your house. In each room, do two things:

1. Thank God for good times in that room with your husband (i.e. kitchen: laughter around the table).

2. Pray over a conflict or problem in your relationship found in that room (i.e. conflict over who cleans up after each meal).

Evaluating My Views

To take steps to protect our marriages and to close the doors on opportunity for infidelity, we must first keep our relationship with God a priority. Second, we must make our relationship with our husband the priority it should be. Answer these "priority" questions by ranking them from 1 to 10 in the order of their importance to you during an average week. (Don't rank them according to how they *should* be, but according to how they really are now.)

_____ Watching my favorite TV show   _____ Reading a page-turning novel

_____ Having a serious talk with my husband about finances   _____ Having a romantic date with my husband

_____ Attending a parent-teacher conference   _____ Preparing for a Bible study group or Sunday school class

_____ Exercising   _____ Shopping

_____ Having a Quiet Time   _____ Cleaning my house

These activities all have an important place in our lives. But sometimes we fail to consciously decide what place of priority each should have. Consequently, we let less important activities crowd out the essential ones.

Finding God's Perspective

1. How can Psalm 103:15,16 and 90:12 help us gain God's perspective on our life?

2. What is God's perspective on the importance of guarding and caring for our marriage (Ephesians 5:31–33; Song of Solomon 2:1–6)?

3. What is the first step to guarding our marriage (Proverbs 3:5–7; Joshua 23:8)?

4. Then what action does Nehemiah show us about being proactive in dealing with temptation (Nehemiah 13:15–21)?

5. What does James 4:17 tell us about a woman who chooses to disregard the importance of re-establishing and guarding the purity of her marriage, whether emotionally or physically?

Checking My Heart

Now go through the list on the previous page once again and rank these items according to what you believe God would want them to be for your life.

Allowing God to Transform Me

Ask God to help you and your husband rearrange your priorities so that you begin to build walls of protection around your marriage and close the door on opportunities for sin. Purpose to talk with your husband immediately, demonstrating your obedience to God.

Lesson 5
"Caring For Your Marriage"

Reading: Review chapter 17.

Spending Time with God

While England received a pounding during World War II, Winston Churchill rallied his country with a rousing call to persevere. For them, there could be only one option: "Victory at all costs, victory in spite of all terror, victory however long and hard the road may be; for without victory there is no survival."[2] The same holds true for us as believers. In Christ we *can* be victorious, no matter how hard and long the battles may be—including the constant assaults on our marriages.

Are you feeling weary from the battle of building a strong marriage? Memorize or place Romans 8:37 in a conspicuous spot: *"But in all these things we overwhelmingly conquer through Him who loved us."* Continually recall this verse to help you remain strong and faithful. Thank the Lord that in our weaknesses, *He* is strong (2 Corinthians 12:9).

Evaluating My Views

Chapter 17 talks about recognizing our needs, because the one who meets our needs is the one with whom we will fall in love. Meeting needs in a marriage works both ways. We must be willing to see and meet our husband's needs as well as desiring him to meet some of ours. Recognizing our needs is not an excuse for selfishness because selfishness *always* has a victim. Someone always pays the price when our focus rests upon ourselves. Others cannot possibly meet all our needs. They weren't meant to! Yet as long as we focus solely on our needs, we will always be taking from others instead of giving—our husbands included. Only as we humble ourselves, yield our lives to Christ, and trust *God* to meet our needs can we minister and give to others as He calls us to do.

Take a few minutes to assess your "need" attitude:

• Do I desire to give as well as to receive?

• Am I seeking to minister to my husband, or just trying to get what I want out of the relationship?

• In what ways can I discover and minister to my husband's needs?

Finding God's Perspective

Charles Swindoll writes: "Our ultimate goal, our highest calling in life is to glorify God—not to be happy. Let that sink in! Glorifying Him is our greatest pursuit. Not to get our way. Not to be comfortable. Not to find fulfillment. Not even to be loved or to be appreciated or to be taken care of. Now these are important, but they are not primary. As I glorify Him, He sees to it that other essential needs are met . . . or my need for them diminishes. Believe me, this concept will change your entire perspective on yourself, your life, and your marriage."[3]

Since glorifying God is to be your greatest pursuit, one of the main ways to do so is by protecting your marriage so that it brings honor to Him. Chapter 17 gives seven ways to protect your marriage. How are you doing in each? Give an example of how you can strengthen each area:

1. Identifying my unmet needs (Song of Solomon 6:3).

2. Spending exclusive time with my husband (Song of Solomon 7:10).

3. Caring about my appearance (Song of Solomon 2:14).

4. Laughing together (Philippians 4:4).

5. Acting like a duck (Philippians 4:6,7).

6. Harboring no unresolved anger against my husband (Ephesians 4:26,27).

7. Praying together with my husband (Matthew 18:20).

Checking My Heart

The following questions are meant to help you identify areas of concern in your marriage. Write out your answers:

1. Are my children more important to me than my husband and our marriage? How can I make my husband and our relationship the priority God desires?

2. Are there issues so deep in our marriage that we need to seek professional counseling before disaster strikes? What are they? What steps do we need to take now so we can begin to resolve these and protect our marriage?

3. What relationships and activities do I have with other men in which I find fulfillment? How can these interfere with my husband exclusively being my best friend and companion? What could be the result?

4. In the seven areas of protecting our marriage listed above in "Finding God's Perspective," which ones do I need to focus on improving? What do I need to do to encourage those changes?

Allowing God to Transform Me

Ask God to give you the strength and wisdom to follow through with the action points written above. Begin now to take the necessary steps to make your husband the priority he should be in your life, thereby building the first wall of protection around your marriage.

Note: If you will *not* be meeting with a discussion group or with another person to go through the Discussion Guide, please turn now to page 133 and go through the questions and new material for Week Six as if it were another daily lesson. You won't want to miss the additional insights found there!

Personal Study
Week Seven
Establishing Accountability and Protective Walls

Lesson 1
"Accountability to God and to My Husband"

Reading: chapter 18

Spending Time with God

We have talked about our desperate need for the Lord every day—that we have no good besides Him and can accomplish nothing of eternal value apart from Him. Nothing can take the place of yielding our lives daily to God's will. And God also tells us that we need one another to help us in a steadfast walk with Christ.

As you prepare to focus on accountability issues in these next few lessons, start by renewing your commitment and accountability to God. Read these verses and pray them back to God for your own life:

> Deuteronomy 10:20,21 – *"You shall fear the Lord your God; you shall serve Him and cling to Him, and you shall swear by His name. He is your praise and He is your God, who has done these great and awesome things for you which your eyes have seen."*

> Jeremiah 24:7 – *"I will give them a heart to know Me, for I am the Lord; and they will be My people, and I will be their God, for they will return to Me with their whole heart."*

Evaluating My Views

To walk faithfully and consistently with the Lord, we must admit that there is no way we can do so on our own. We need Christ's Spirit to work through us, and we need the body of Christ as well. As Chinese pastor Brother Yun said, "It is not great men who change the world, but weak men in the hands of a great God."[1]

Ask yourself:

1. In what ways am I weak and vulnerable to the enemy's temptations?

2. What areas of my life do I try to hide from God? From my husband?

3. What would need to happen for me to be completely honest with my husband?

Finding God's Perspective

1. According to 1 Samuel 16:7 and Matthew 10:26, why is it so essential to be truthful with God?

2. What are the results of being honest with God (Psalm 24:3–5)?

Many women fear that honesty will destroy their marital relationship. But what's *really* frightening is to think that a marriage foundation rests upon secrets and lies. As long as secrets and lies lurk within a marriage, an invisible wall separates the spouses from the intimacy God designed for them to have within their marriage.

Dr. Willard Harley writes: "I believe that honesty is so essential to the success of marriage, that hiding past infidelity makes a marriage dishonest, preventing emotional closeness and intimacy. It isn't honesty that causes the pain; it's the affair. Honesty is simply revealing truth to the victim . . . It's patronizing to think that a spouse cannot bear to hear the truth. Anyone who assumes that their spouse cannot handle truth is being incredibly disrespectful, manipulative, and in the final analysis, dangerous. How little you must think of your spouse when you try to protect him or her from the truth."[2]

Of course the initial shock of learning about a partner's past failure(s) is very painful. But few divorces actually occur because of such honesty. Rather, honesty becomes the groundwork upon which the marriage is rebuilt. This honors God, and allows the relationship to finally grow to a depth never previously experienced.

3. What does God say He desires in all our relationships, of which our marriage is the *most* important (Ephesians 4:24,25)?

Checking My Heart

1. How much exclusive time have you begun to spend with your husband each week?

2. How will implementing the No Secrets Policy with your husband change your marriage?

3. In which area of your marriage will it be the most difficult to re-establish honesty?

Remember, the No Secrets Policy does not mean sharing every thought that pops into your head. For instance, saying to your husband something like, "Honey, I have to be honest; what used to be your chest now seems to be resting around your waist" is not honesty—that's cruelty said without the love of Christ. The No Secrets Policy relates to any area in *your* life that affects your relationship with your husband.

Allowing God to Transform Me

Pray that God will bury the truth of Psalm 32:2 in your heart: "*Blessed is the man. . . in whose spirit is no deceit*" (NIV). Ask God to give you the strength to establish the No Secrets Policy with your husband. This is one of the strongest walls you can build around your marriage. It works!

Lesson 2

"Accountability with Mature Christian Women"

Reading: Review chapter 18 from the section titled "Accountability with Mature Christian Women" to the end of the chapter.

Spending Time with God

God wrote about the prideful, stubborn Israelites: *"They would not accept my counsel, they spurned all my reproof. So they shall eat of the fruit of their own way and be satiated with their own devices. For the waywardness of the naïve will kill them, and the complacency of fools will destroy them. But he who listens to me shall live securely and will be at ease from the dread of evil"* (Proverbs 1:30–33).

Ask God to reveal areas in your life where you are resistant to listening to God, your husband, or others.

Evaluating My Views

An article in the *Worldwide Challenge* magazine says, "We need people to help us walk by faith. If Satan can isolate us from the rest of the body, like a wolf singling out a wounded lamb, it's easier for him to make the kill."[3]

1. What do you think of the statement: "If there's something in my life I don't want anyone to know, someone *needs* to know"?

2. Name one or two mature Christian women in whom you could confide and turn to for godly wisdom and accountability.

   If you don't know anyone who fits the criteria for an accountability partner, ask the Lord to lead you to someone. You could start by asking your Bible study leader or your pastor and his wife to suggest a godly woman in the church.

3. How might pride keep you from setting up accountability with a friend?

Finding God's Perspective

1. What principle does Ecclesiastes 4:9,10 give us about accountability?

2. How does Proverbs 13:20 help us with the kind of accountability partner we should select?

3. Consider the four qualities of accountability:
   - Be teachable—How does Proverbs 5:12–14 motivate you to be teachable?

   - Be vulnerable—How does Psalm 38:9 help you to be vulnerable?

   - Be honest—According to Psalm 51:6, how deeply does God desire honesty to go in our lives?

   - Be dependable—How will God reward the faithful (Psalm 31:23)?

Checking My Heart

1. In which accountability area is honesty the most difficult for you? (Circle one.)

Accountability with God

Accountability with your husband

Accountability with a close friend

2. What mature Christian woman will you immediately call to set up a regular weekly accountability time? (Or who will you immediately seek out to help you find a mature, godly accountability partner?)

3. Write out the specific questions you would like your accountability partner to ask you each week:

Allowing God to Transform Me

Write below the changes that you desire to see in your marriage by having an accountability partner. Ask God to give you the discipline to follow through in making accountability a reality in your life.

Please don't let this day go by without setting up an accountability relationship! If the enemy can keep us from being accountable, he is far more able to keep things in the dark corners of our lives where they can grow and multiply. As Charles Swindoll said in *Living Above the Level of Mediocrity*, "People who really make an impact model accountability."[4] That can be you!

Lesson 3
"Protecting Your Marriage through Daily Time with God"

Reading: chapter 19

Spending Time with God

No stage of life guarantees immunity from falling into sin. Age and spiritual maturity provide no guarantee against infidelity, even if it has never been a struggle in your marriage up to now. Whether young or old, we are always susceptible, and therefore must always guard our lives and our marriages. We are all one step away from making some horrible decision. Therefore, we need to cling to God daily for His protection and strength.

God promised the Israelite people that He would build them a protective wall against their enemies (Psalm 125:2). God is also actively protecting us. He gives us a wonderful picture of His protection in Psalm 91. Read all of Psalm 91 and list the ways God protects us as we cling to Him.

Evaluating My Views

Picture your marriage as being a magnificent castle with a wall around it. That wall protects your marriage castle from the world's desire to destroy it through immoral influences. See if your marriage castle has the protection it needs:

• Do you have breaches in your protective wall? What are they?

• What influences are you allowing into your home that are silently eroding the foundation of your marriage?

• What "good" activities are keeping you from spending time building your relationship with your husband?

• What kind of time are you giving to God and His Word each day so that His Word can teach, reprove, correct, and train you in righteousness (2 Timothy 3:16)?

Finding God's Perspective

In a recent study of Christian leaders—both male and female who had fallen into immorality—one pattern frequently emerged: They resisted examining their lives and confronting the sin that was spreading like a cancerous growth within them. The problem areas in their lives were as diverse as having a proud egotistical nature, to refusing accountability, to resisting authority. But whatever the issue, these fallen leaders had opposed an examination of their lives, and they ended up in adultery.

1. What does Proverbs 16:6 say will keep us from sin?

2. How does coming to God's Word protect our marriage (Galatians 5:16,17; Titus 2:11,12)?

3. Knowing this, why is it so critical that we come to His Word *every day* in order to protect our marriage (Hebrews 3:12,13)?

Checking My Heart

The *most* important protection you can give your marriage is to stay broken, humble, and dependent on the Lord. And the only way to do that is to spend daily time with God and time in His Word. Read the following verses and give one specific way you can apply each to building your relationship with your husband:

• Psalm 119:28 – *"My soul weeps because of grief; strengthen me according to Your word."*

• Psalm 119:30 – *"I have chosen the faithful way; I have placed Your ordinances before me."*

• Psalm 119:37 – *"Turn my eyes away from worthless things; preserve my life according to your word"* (NIV).

• Psalm 119:54 – *"Your decrees are the theme of my song wherever I lodge"* (NIV).

Allowing God to Transform Me

As we stay in a right relationship with God, we will also make right decisions related to our marriage. But it all begins with our dependence on the Lord. Ask God to help you put into practice the truths you learned from Psalm 119 above. As you go about your day, practice these precepts. If you are having difficulty in an area, stop right then and read the verse addressing the problem. Then ask God to keep you faithful in applying His Word to your life.

Lesson 4
"Protecting Your Marriage: Other Men and the Workplace"

Reading: Review in chapter 19 the sections titled "Protecting Your Marriage by Safeguarding Your Relationships with Other Men" and "Protecting Your Marriage through Boundaries in the Workplace."

Spending Time with God

Read the story in 2 Samuel 11:1–12:14 of how David became entangled in adultery. Then ask God to show you ways that you may be opening the door for temptation without even realizing you are doing so.

Evaluating My Views

Go back through 2 Samuel 11:1–4 and write all the steps that David took before he actually committed the act of adultery. Notice how the temptation turned into a process of one sin leading to another and another.

Do you find yourself in a process of decisions leading toward sin? If so, how can you stop the progression to sin?

Remember, *"Whatever is not from faith is sin"* (Romans 14:23).

Finding God's Perspective

Psalm 51 is David's lament after his sin with Bathsheba. Read Psalm 51 and answer the questions:

1. At whom does David say his sin is directed (verse 4)?

2. Who is the only one who can cleanse David from his sin (verses 7–10)?

3. What does God desire the most from us to guard us from giving in to sin (verse 16,17)?

Checking My Heart

Psalm 119:9 instructs us, *"How can a young man keep his way pure? By keeping it according to Your word."* God's words and wisdom guide us into maintaining integrity and purity in every facet of every relationship. Yet if we are not careful, a friendship or a working relationship with another man can easily grow beyond the boundaries God intended. That is why we must *predetermine* our actions in all our relationships. In chapter 19 of the book, we looked at two important ways to protect our marriage:

• Safeguarding our relationships with other men
• Building boundaries in the workplace

Which of the ideas in those two sections of chapter 19 do you need to implement in your own life? (Feel free to refer back to the book.) Write these down, along with the specific steps you will take to carry out these safeguards:

Ideas I Need To Implement	How I Will Do So

Allowing God to Transform Me

The key to protecting your marriage is to remain instantly sensitive and obedient to the Holy Spirit. God's Spirit within us will give us warning signals, but if we choose to ignore them, our heart quickly becomes insensitive to His flashing red lights. Begin implementing the safeguards He has shown you above. Ask Him to make you sensitive to other ways you may be allowing a breach in your "invisible wall" toward other men. As you choose to obey Him immediately, you will marvel at your increasing sensitivity toward His Spirit.

Lesson 5
"Protecting Your Marriage through What You Wear, See, Hear, and Do"

Reading: Review chapter 19 from the section entitled "Protecting Your Marriage through Discretion in Clothing" to the end of the chapter

Spending Time with God

King Asa began his reign of Judah well. Yet like David, Solomon, and many others in Scripture, he became an example of caving in to sin in his later years (2 Chronicles 14–16). God gave us these examples as warnings for our own lives. *"Now these things happened to them as an example, and they were written for our instruction"* (1 Corinthians 10:11). We can crumble just as easily in the face of temptation. Pray through Psalm 51:10, asking God to help you purify your mind and actions as you go through this lesson: *"Create in me a clean heart, O God, and renew a steadfast spirit within me."*

Evaluating My Views

Consider each of the following areas. Are you using any of them inappropriately? Are they influencing you away from marital faithfulness in any way? How? Write down your answers beside each area:

What I wear—

What I see—

What I hear—

What I do on the Internet—

Finding God's Perspective

1. What is God's perspective on the way we are to dress (1 Timothy 2:9,10)?

2. What can we do when we are tempted visually by something (Psalm 16:8)?

3. What warning do we find in Psalm 81:11,12 about what can happen when we listen to that which hardens our heart toward God?

4. How does purity apply to our "private" use of the Internet (Psalm 139:3)?

Checking My Heart

Check the areas that need strengthening in order to protect your marriage:

☐ Are you practicing safeguards in all your relationships with other men by:
  Including your husband's name in all conversations?
  Having your husband meet the other men in your life?
  Getting to know the other wives?
  Practicing the "invisible wall"?
  Avoiding/ending all private and personal conversations with other men?
  Never giving another man a "signal" that you find him interesting?
  Avoiding hugging, kissing, and dancing with another man?
  Practicing the No Secrets Policy with your husband when you feel drawn toward another man?
☐ Are you dressing and acting with "*purity and reverence*," adorning yourself "*with proper clothing, modestly and discreetly*"?
☐ Are you guarding your eyes and ears against anything God considers vile and impure, as well as anything that entices your mind toward romantic fantasies outside the bounds of your marriage?
☐ Are you sharing things by e-mail or in a chat room with another man that you are not sharing with your husband? Are you allowing someone to provide emotional fulfillment over the Internet that should be coming from your husband?

Allowing God to Transform Me

Ask God to help you carry out each of the areas you marked above. If you have not yet begun to implement the No Secrets Policy and establish weekly time to spend alone with your husband, now's the time! It would be wise to discuss the above issues with him. As you do so, the walls of protection around your marriage will continue to grow stronger.

Note: If you will *not* be meeting with a discussion group or with another person to go through the Discussion Guide, please turn now to page 136 and go through the questions and new material for Week Seven as if it were another daily lesson. You won't want to miss the additional insights found there!

Lesson 1
"Feelings, Secrets, the Adrenaline Rush, and Curiosity"

Reading: chapter 20

Spending Time with God

Jesus faced greater temptations than we have ever known. Satan directly challenged Jesus in all the areas where the flesh is susceptible. Read Matthew 4:1–11, and thank God for the example Jesus set in resisting Satan's lies.

Evaluating My Views

We all possess "chinks in our armor" that open up opportunities for infidelity. Yet often we are unaware that these cracks in our walls of defense even exist. Therefore, we need to stay alert to possible dangers in order to avoid giving in when temptation strikes.

Chapter 20 gives us some of the most common temptations that can break down the sacredness of our marriage vows. The following are the first four things mentioned that you should never do when you feel drawn to another man. Consider each carefully, and write down scenarios in your life where you may be vulnerable and could choose to go against the principle mentioned.

1. Don't divulge your feelings.

2. Don't keep secrets.

3. Don't be lured in by the adrenaline rush.

4. Don't give in to curiosity.

Finding God's Perspective

Given the lack of restraint in relationships these days, we may easily find ourselves sharing personally with another man. But those seeds of intimacy can quickly germinate and grow into an improper emotional relationship. That's why we must predetermine our responses to a temptation.

1. What does Psalm 141:3 tell us to do when we sense intimacy developing with another man?

2. Some women may be drawn toward the forbidden by the adrenaline rush of having an exhilarating secret. Others may simply be lured in by curiosity. How can Colossians 3:2,3 help with these temptations?

3. What do you need to do the moment you confront any of these temptations (Proverbs 27:12)?

Checking My Heart

1. In Week 2, we talked about the need to never underestimate the lure of attraction toward another man. What does "never underestimate the power of attraction" mean to you now?

2. How will you extinguish the sparks of attraction if you are struggling with any of these temptations?

3. What boundaries have you preset that will help keep you from sharing personal thoughts and feelings with another man?

Allowing God to Transform Me

One of the most heartening promises for Christians is found in 1 Corinthians 10:13. Memorize this verse, and ask God to help you practice His *"way of escape"* for every temptation. Remember to live from the inside out, practicing the Spirit-controlled life, calling on His power to flee any temptation of attraction toward another man.

Lesson 2
"Flirting, Fantasizing, Rescuing, and Doubting"

Reading: Review chapter 20 from the section titled "Don't Flirt" through "Don't Doubt Scripture or God."

Spending Time with God

As we know, God desires our lives to be holy in every aspect. Living in His holiness protects us and our marriage. Yet we can so easily let "little" areas slip by. Romans 13:14 reminds us of our daily need to *"put on the Lord Jesus Christ, and make no provision for the flesh in regard to its lust."* If you haven't done so yet, "put on Christ" again today, asking Him to reveal any areas in your life that He desires to expose as you go through this lesson.

Evaluating My Views

In Lesson 1 of this Session, you evaluated four areas in which you may be susceptible to certain types of temptations when drawn to another man. Now let's evaluate the last four areas. Write down any scenarios where you may be vulnerable to responding in one of these destructive ways, thereby causing a breach in the wall around your marriage castle.

5. Don't flirt.

6. Don't fantasize.

7. Don't give in to rescue tendencies.

8. Don't doubt Scripture or God.

Finding God's Perspective

If "Flirting 101" were offered for women at a university, the course enrollment would be zero—we women *already* know how! No one needs to tell Susie how to get Johnny's attention. That savvy got built into her genes! Most women so easily and naturally flirt that many Christian women don't even consciously realize how they come across to men. But the men do!

1. What does Proverbs 10:10 say about flirting?

2. Rather than allowing our minds to daydream and fantasize, what should we do (Philippians 4:8)?

Often a woman flirts to get attention and to feed her ego. Feeding the ego is similar to feeding needs of self worth. Both show that we are looking to others to try and feel good about who we are. Those needs can truly be fulfilled only in Christ. He knows our needs, our heart cries, and our yearnings for love and affection. He alone is able to satisfy our deepest longings and to fill our hearts with His love and tender mercies. But if we try and find others to meet our needs of self worth, those desires become an open door for the first kind male who offers us special attention.

3. What does the Lord say about meeting our needs in Isaiah 58:11?

4. According to 2 Corinthians 11:3, what should the focus of our life be?

Checking My Heart

1. Which of the eight improper responses presents the greatest challenge to you in your interaction with other men? (If needed, look back at Lesson 1 to remind yourself of the first four improper responses.)

2. In this particular area, name at least three specific ways you could respond that would please the Lord and fortify the walls of protection around your marriage.

3. Hebrews 2:18 tells us, *"For since He Himself was tempted in that which He has suffered, He is able to come to the aid of those who are tempted."* According to this verse, what is the hope that we have in the midst of all our temptations?

Allowing God to Transform Me

The apostle Peter ends his second letter in the Bible with admonition and encouragement for us all: *"You therefore . . . be on your guard so that you are not carried away by the error of unprincipled men and fall from your own steadfastness, but grow in the grace and knowledge of our Lord and Savior Jesus Christ. To Him be the glory, both now and to the day of eternity. Amen"* (2 Peter 3:17,18).

God alone can strengthen us to walk victoriously. Therefore, we must cling to Him in utter dependence each day. Continue to practice Dying, Adoring, Confessing, and Arming daily so that you will *"grow in the grace and knowledge of our Lord and Savior Jesus Christ."* To Him be all glory!

Lesson 3
"Seven Immediate Steps for Responding to Marital Temptation"

Reading: Review in chapter 20 the section titled "Seven Immediate Steps for Responding to Marital Temptation."

Spending Time with God

Second Peter 2:9 gives us great encouragement: *"The Lord knows how to rescue the godly from temptation."* We can rest in knowing that we have a loving God who is quite able to deliver us from every tempting situation. Thank God for His promise to deliver you from all temptation. Be specific about temptations you face.

Evaluating My Views

Chapter 20 gives us seven immediate steps for responding to marital temptation. These steps are invaluable when your heart suddenly feels drawn to some other man. When you find yourself in such a situation, you must have a plan for getting out! Predetermining what to do can make all the difference between righteousness and disaster.

Think of a situation in your past (or present) when you felt attracted to another man. Go through these seven steps and write how you should have responded in the situation. (If you can't think of a particular situation, then go through the seven steps and write how you would respond if a situation occurred in your life today.)

1. Flee! Get away from the person! (How would you do this?)

2. Pray for God's perspective on infidelity and your marriage. (Write out your prayer.)

3. Resist the devil. (What would you say?)

4. Tell your husband. (Write what you would say.)

5. Tell your accountability partner. (Write out the questions you would want her to ask you.)

6. Replace enticing mental pictures of another man with Scripture. (List a few verses.)

7. Do whatever it takes! (Write anything else you would do.)

Finding God's Perspective

To be transformed more and more into Christ's likeness, we must resist temptation. If we don't, sin will overwhelm our lives and we will not only lose the joy and peace of our Christian walk, but we will also reap the consequences of our actions. The following verses give Scriptural principles of resisting temptation. Write what these verses tell us to do:

1. Proverbs 1:10

2. Proverbs 4:14,15

3. Psalm 86:7

4. Romans 6:12,13

Checking My Heart

Just as we exercise our muscles to maintain their strength, we must practice instant obedience in dealing with temptations so that we will grow more like Christ. And the more we practice, the quicker we become at obeying the Lord.

Remember, every decision bears consequences. By our choices, we either build our homes for the Lord, or we tear them apart with our own hands (Proverbs 14:1). So when any temptation arises toward another man, immediately practice the seven steps above to extinguish those sparks.

What are you willing to do to hold your marriage in highest honor and to keep your marriage bed pure? Write down your plan of action:

Allowing God to Transform Me

Write out these seven steps on a card that you can take with you in your purse. Refer to these steps in times of temptation and practice them immediately. Proverbs 16:17 says, *"The highway of the upright is to depart from evil."* Make fleeing from temptation such a common practice in your life that your path away from sin looks like an eight-lane freeway! Predetermine before God right now that you will do whatever it takes to keep your marriage sacred.

Lesson 4
"Commitment to Protecting Your Marriage"
Reading: Review chapter 20.

Spending Time with God

God is always there to give us His strength in the midst of any temptation. If we try to rely on our own power, we will continually fall. He alone is our Rock and our Deliverer.

Read Psalm 62:5–8 and thank God for providing the strength to persevere.

Evaluating My Views

Read Hebrews 12:1. What does this mean regarding marital temptations? It means realizing your weakness when you are tempted and acknowledging your need to cling desperately to the Lord each and every day, dying on His altar and choosing the Spirit-controlled life. It means starting *now* to care for your marriage, rekindling the tenderness between you and your husband. It means setting up accountability, both with your husband and with another woman. It means immediately practicing the seven steps that extinguish the sparks of attraction toward another man. It means making predetermined decisions about how you'll act around other men. It means practicing integrity in what you wear, see, hear, and in *everything* you do.

1. Name one encumbrance that entangles you and affects your marriage.

2. What is this encumbrance doing to your relationship with your husband?

3. What is the likely outcome if you don't deal with this problem?

Finding God's Perspective

1. As we choose to demonstrate God's holiness and integrity in our lives and marriages, what is the result (Matthew 5:16)?

2. Choosing to walk in obedience and holiness is not always easy. In 1 Peter 5:8-10, what does God tell us can happen as we obey?

3. What is the result of our endurance (James 1:2-4, 2 Corinthians 4:17)?

Checking My Heart

Read 2 Timothy 4:7,8. God's magnificent promises stand before us. Because of this, it is *always* worth the effort to endure and to do whatever it takes to walk in holiness. And such choices *will* protect our marriages! Therefore, please go before God and make the following commitment to resist temptation and remain pure in your marriage relationship:

- I am determined to do whatever it takes to hold my marriage in honor and to keep our marriage bed undefiled.
- I choose not to underestimate the power of attraction to another man, and will immediately practice the seven steps to extinguish any sparks of attraction.
- I have predetermined not to share with another man any feelings I may have toward him.
- I have predetermined not to spend inappropriate or secret time with another man.
- I have predetermined to guard against building intimate, emotional relationships with men other than my husband.
- I have determined to live by the No Secrets Policy with my husband.
- I have asked the Lord to show me any areas that constitute flirting in my manner toward other men, and I am immediately changing my behavior with the strength of Christ.
- I daily practice *"taking every thought captive to the obedience of Christ"* and therefore guard against allowing my mind to fantasize or daydream about time with another man.
- I have predetermined to send all hurting men to another man for counsel and help.
- I have chosen to trust God and His Word regardless of any current questions or doubts I may have.

Signed _____ *Date* _____

Allowing God to Transform Me

If you have not yet made this commitment, then please ask the Lord to make you willing to do *whatever it takes* to guard your marriage. Though a temptation may look enticing, the goal of the Tempter is *always* to steal your peace, your joy, your usefulness, your family, and your life. Giving in to sin is *never, ever* worth it! Predetermining righteousness is worth everything!

Lesson 5
"You Can Make a Difference"

Reading: chapter 21.

Spending Time with God

Picture standing before Christ *"in the presence of His glory blameless with great joy"* (Jude 24), having received what was promised for your faithfulness (Hebrews 10:36). Imagine how satisfied you will feel standing before Jesus knowing that you have obeyed Him in keeping your most important earthly relationship pure. You cannot control your husband's responses—and God will not hold you responsible for his sin—but you can bring your own fleshly nature under the Spirit's control.

Read Matthew 13:43 and 2 Timothy 4:8. Spend a moment giving praise to God. We owe Him everything!

Evaluating My Views

Now that you have completed this course, where do you stand? Take an evaluation by looking at the truths we have studied on the left-hand side, and fill in the right-hand side with your response:

Truth	Is this true in my life? If not, what needs to happen?
I am absolutely committed to abstaining from any form of infidelity (emotional and physical), and to honoring my marriage vows till death do us part.	
I believe that apart from Christ, I have "no good thing" (Psalm 16:2) and can do nothing of eternal value (John 15:5).	
This belief drives me in utter dependence *each day* to lay my life on His altar, to spend time in His Word, time in prayer, and to put on His protective armor.	
I am choosing to live the Spirit-controlled life moment by moment, practicing transparent repentance, and choosing to let the inside (Spirit) dominate the outside (flesh).	
I have restored a clear conscience by asking for forgiveness from anyone alive "that I have ever wronged, offended, or hurt in any way." [1]	

Truth	Is this true in my life? If not, what needs to happen?
I am choosing to obey immediately all that God shows me.	
I am choosing integrity in every aspect of my life, both inside my home and outside, including what I allow to enter my eyes and ears.	
I am growing in practicing godly, sacrificial love toward my husband and others, choosing not to depend upon my feelings.	
I am caring for my marriage by spending exclusive time each week with my husband.	
I have established accountability by committing to the No Secrets Policy with my husband, and also by communicating regularly with a mature Christian woman.	
If I have been involved with another man, I have cut off all contact, told my husband, and set up accountability in order to restore faithfulness.	
I am safeguarding my relationships with all other men by maintaining an "invisible wall" between us and by taking actions so as not to build intimate, emotional relationships with them.	
I have predetermined to practice the seven steps when drawn to another man, and will not share my feelings with him, nor flirt, fantasize, etc.	

Answer the following questions:

1. As a result of this study, my marriage has changed in these ways:

2. My relationship with God has changed in these ways:

3. The most important step(s) I am taking to build and protect my marriage is:

4. Now that I have gone through this study, two other women whose lives and marriages would greatly benefit by going through this study with me are:

Finding God's Perspective

Read Proverbs 18:22, Proverbs 19:14 and Proverbs 31:10,11. Write a thank-you to God for how you are a living example of these verses:

Checking My Heart

Chapter 21 says, "Life is full of peaks and valleys. The daily, hourly choices of making right decisions to climb the hill called 'righteousness' can be difficult. It's often hard to turn away from an enticing temptation. Sometimes it really hurts! But in the end, it's definitely worth the *prize of the upward call of God in Christ Jesus'* (Philippians 3:14)."

Are you determined to be the light of Christ in this generation? Ask God to guide you in writing a statement of commitment to Jesus that includes giving Him your time, talents, and marriage. Use this as your mission statement for your future. You *can* make a difference!

Allowing God to Transform Me

As you end this study, determine to follow through on the areas that need change which you identified in "Evaluating My Views." Praise God that He is committed to working wonders in our lives! *"Blessed be the Lord God, the God of Israel, who alone works wonders. And blessed be His glorious name forever; and may the whole earth be filled with His glory. Amen, and Amen"* (Psalm 72:18,19).

To Him be all glory and praise!

Note: If you will *not* be meeting with a discussion group or with another person to go through the Discussion Guide, please turn now to page 139 and go through the questions and new material for Week Eight as if it were another daily lesson. You won't want to miss the additional insights found there!

Discussion Guide

"He who began a good work in you will
perfect it until the day of Christ Jesus."
Philippians 1:6

Discussion Guide
Week One Conversation

Opening Discussion

Spend a few moments doing introductions. As an icebreaker, have each woman describe one non-intimate, humorous incident in her marriage.

Read aloud these few basic rules that group members should follow:

- All personal information brought up in the group **must be held in strictest confidence** by all other group members.

- When an individual desires to share personal and private matters concerning her husband, the issue of honoring and respecting our spouse is vital—even if the marriage is a difficult one. Therefore, each member should consider talking with her husband and, if possible, receiving his permission beforehand to share such things. Again, this information *must* be kept in strictest confidence within the group. Our goal is to *build* marriages. Sharing outside the group will only bring damage.

- Each person must be affirmed as valuable to God and to the group no matter what has happened in her past.

- All answers to questions and other responses are to be given respect. There are no foolish questions or answers.

- No one is required to share personal information with the group.

Discussion Time

(Note: **Instructions for you as facilitator are in bold type.** Material to say aloud during group time is in regular type. Material included in boxes is extra material to use during the discussion time if you desire.)

1. What do you think is the most difficult problem our society faces in supporting the institution of marriage?

2. How do you think society's views influence married Christian women today?

Throughout the Bible, we find illustrations of how easily we can all fall into temptation and sin, starting with the very first man and woman, going all the way through the book of Revelation. Adam and Eve actually walked and talked with God, experiencing a divine closeness that we can't imagine until heaven, yet they blatantly defied God. And within one generation, their son Cain had descended to committing murder!

Giving in to temptation can happen so easily. How quickly Eve chose to eat the very fruit God had instructed them to resist. How quickly Cain's anger erupted toward His brother and he committed murder. How quickly King David chose to lust, then committed adultery and murder. Apart from God's grace, that same propensity toward sin resides in each of us. If we are not on guard and in prayer every day, desperately seeking Christ to keep us faithful and obedient, it can happen just as quickly to us.

3. Consider Judy's story in the book. What choices did she make that ensnared her in a compromising relationship?

Dennis Rainey, president of FamilyLife ministries, says: "Emotional adultery is unfaithfulness of the heart. It starts when two people of the opposite sex begin talking with each other about intimate struggles, doubts, or feelings. They start sharing their souls in a way that God intended exclusively for the marriage relationship. Emotional adultery is friendship with the opposite sex that goes too far."[1]

4. Why is emotional infidelity so damaging?

Christian author and clinical psychologist Dr. Willard Harley writes: "We are all wired to have an affair. We can all fall in love with someone of the opposite sex if that person meets one of our emotional needs. If you don't think it can happen to you because of your conviction or will-power, you are particularly vulnerable to an affair."[2]

5. How do you respond to Dr. Harley's quote?

6. **Read Mark 10:5–9.** What are the principles of marriage that Jesus gives us?

7. **Have different women read: Hebrews 13:4; Exodus 20:14; and 1 Thessalonians 4:3,7,8.** What do these verses have in common?

8. How does infidelity affect our children?

Living a faithful, godly life in our homes greatly impacts the upcoming generation. The Lord gives us an encouraging illustration of how we as godly wives can have a powerful influence on our children. In 2 Timothy, Paul gives us a peek through the window of Timothy's home.

Timothy's father was most likely an unbeliever, yet Timothy learned Old Testament Scriptures and possessed a sincere faith from his childhood. Where did this come from? Mom and Grandma! Timothy's mother and grandmother were believers, and they saw to his spiritual instruction (2 Timothy 1:5; 3:14,15). Since the vast majority of believers come to Christ before the age of eighteen, mothers have a significant role to play in the next generation's spiritual heritage!

9. Why is a marriage worth saving even if the wife hasn't been faithful to her husband?

Astronaut Charlie Duke flew to the moon, yet his marriage was sinking below ground. "'Our story really is the power of God to heal relationships,' Charlie says. 'I don't care how broken a relationship is; Jesus can heal it if we are humble and seek God's will. It's been a tremendously exciting adventure as we walk with the Lord as a couple and see God's hand in our marriage as He saved us from the divorce court.'"[3]

The Bible considers marriage as a covenant or a life-long pledge. Kay Coles James, director of the U.S. Office of Personnel Management, says, "After I realized marriage meant forever, my marriage flourished. Forever is not a ball and chain; it is a concept that enables us to truly enjoy the freedom of commitment. It is the cornerstone of marriage."[4]

10. Why is it so important that we consider our marriage vows as permanent?

From God's perspective, our marriages are a symbol to the world of Christ's relationship with His bride, which is the church. Therefore, He requires us to guard and protect our marriages, not only for our own sakes, but also for a watching world.

Prayer Time

Each week, the group will spend time praying for one another. This week, pray for each other's marriage relationships.

Allow group members to mention their prayer requests. Then ask for volunteers to pray for each request. Encourage group members to keep a list of prayer concerns in their workbook so that they can pray for each other between sessions. However, in recording anything personal use the person's initials or no name at all to protect their privacy.

Discussion Guide
Week Two Conversation

Opening Discussion

Give each woman a slip of paper and make sure everyone has a pencil. Print this sentence on your slip of paper without showing anyone what you write:

> The cook makes a big dish in time for the noon meal.

Hand your slip of paper to the person beside you. That person copies the sentence onto her slip of paper, but changes one letter. She can drop a letter, add a letter, or substitute a letter, but the new word she creates must be an actual word, and it doesn't have to make sense within the sentence. For example:

> The **b**ook makes a big dish in time for the noon meal.
> Or
> The cook **t**akes a big dish in time for the noon meal.

Then the next person takes the new slip of paper and changes a letter. For example:

> The book makes a **p**ig dish in time for the noon meal.
> Or
> The cook takes a big dish in **l**ime for the noon meal.

The sentence goes around the circle of women until everyone has had a chance to change a letter. Then have someone read the original sentence and the final, altered sentence. The final sentence will have changed meaning or become hilariously nonsensical.

Discuss these questions:

How does this activity help us understand what happens when we do not tell the truth to our husband?

What are some negative consequences of being deceitful in our marriage?

Discussion Time

(Note: **Instructions for you as facilitator are in bold type.** Material to say aloud during group time is in regular type. Material included in boxes is extra material to use during the discussion time if you desire.)

1. Why is it so important that we heed God's call to turn from our sins (repent)?

Like a loving father seeking to protect his children, God offers us the gift of repentance so that we will turn from our sin and the devastation that it brings. But if we continue to ignore God's gracious offer to repent and turn back to Him, our hearts can become so hardened that we no longer desire to leave the sin. And as we've seen, sin only multiplies into greater sin, becoming a ball and chain that we drag with us through life. What freedom we can experience if we will confess and turn from our sin, breaking the chain that held us captive!

2. **Read Ecclesiastes 5:4.** Why is it so essential to regard your wedding vows as sacred before God?

3. **Read Proverbs 12:20.** What is the contrast found in this verse? How does this apply to a person involved in infidelity?

4. Why is it so important to be honest with yourself first? (**Make sure that the issue of rationalization is addressed here. Talk about how the human mind is able to rationalize any sin, whether it is fantasizing, adultery, or murder. However, God is not a God of excuses, and we are held accountable for our choices and our actions.**)

5. **Read Jeremiah 32:27.** How does being honest with God provide the key for changing wrong behavior?

6. What difference will it make in your time with God if you truly believe that the quality of every relationship in your life depends upon your relationship with the Lord?

7. God's design for marriage is that the two become "one flesh." **Have a volunteer read Matthew 19:4-6.** How does becoming "one flesh" in marriage relate to the No Secrets Policy? (**Do not let your group members get hung up on the No Secrets Policy here. It will be discussed in greater detail during Week Seven. For now, keep emphasizing the need for each person to ask the Lord for willingness to do whatever He desires.**)

The spiritual and emotional aspects of being "one flesh" can only fully be realized in a marriage free of secrets and deceit. The No Secrets Policy, of course, must be accomplished sensitively, in a spirit of humble brokenness over our sin. Because this issue is so important for the intimacy, health, and protection of *any* marriage, we will come back to it at a later time. But for now, keep asking the Lord to make you willing to do whatever He calls you to do for the sake of protecting and building your marriage.

8. What steps should a woman take to cut off all contact with a man with whom she has had an improper relationship, whether emotionally or physically:

At work?
In her neighborhood?
At her church?

9. How are you working to build trust in your marriage relationship?

Prayer Time

Use this time to pray for difficulties group members may be having with maintaining honesty and implementing the No Secrets Policy in their marriage. Steer other members away from giving advice, but instead encourage each other and pray for the specific situations mentioned. Remind group members about the need to **keep all discussions confidential**, and to continue praying for one another throughout the week.

Discussion Guide
Week Three Conversation

Opening Discussion

Discuss how the spiritual walk of each marriage partner affects the marriage relationship. Then have group members explain how each of the following contrasting attitudes plays a part in tearing down or building up a marriage:

Pride/humility
Lust/purity
Condemnation/conviction
Unfaithfulness/commitment

Discussion Time

(Note: **Instructions for you as facilitator are in bold type.** Material to say aloud during group time is in regular type. Material included in boxes is extra material to use during the discussion time if you desire.)

1. Why is a personal relationship with Christ so critical to a marriage?

2. Why do you think Satan tries so hard to destroy marriages?

3. In what ways does pride hinder our walk with God? Give examples from your life.

To stay transparent before God, no act of disobedience is too small to confess. As humans, we would tend to think that Adam and Eve's act of eating a piece of forbidden fruit was a pretty minor infraction. But in God's eyes, it was an act of man exerting his will above God's—the consequences of which affected the entire creation! Every act of disobedience reflects the exact same sin as Adam and Eve's—*pride*.

Pride is the root of every sin under the sun. Pride says, "I want *my* way over God's way." Pride doesn't want me to allow God to be God over *my* life. Pride wants to put *me* in control. Pride wants me to live independently of the Lord. Pride also forgets that whatever God has for me is for my good.

Actually, we have *nothing* of which to be proud! Anything good in us comes solely from the grace of the Lord Jesus. Remember, we were slaves to sin before Christ came to live within us (Romans 6:19). It's only through the work of the Holy Spirit who now resides in us that we can choose righteousness in the first place! Paul reminds us, *"What do you have that you did not receive [from the Lord]?"* (1 Corinthians 4:7). And because we are solely a work of God's grace, Paul also says, *"May it never be that I would boast, except in the cross of our Lord Jesus Christ"* (Galatians 6:14). We are truly a work of His grace from beginning to end.

4. What are the two steps of spiritual breathing used to practice transparent repentance?

5. What difference did practicing transparent repentance make in your life this week?

6. What happened as a result of your steps to establish a clear conscience with others this week?

7. Give an example of Satan's condemnation in your life. Give an example of the Holy Spirit's conviction. What is the difference between the two?

8. What does being *"dead to sin but alive to God in Christ Jesus"* (Romans 6:11) look like in your life?

9. **Read each of the verses and then have a volunteer answer the question.** With your new nature in Christ, how are you to respond to:

• Your flesh (Romans 13:14)?[5]

• Your mind (2 Corinthians 10:5)?[6]

• Your words (Ephesians 4:29)?[7]

• Your marriage (Proverbs 31:10–12)?[8]

• Your children (Deuteronomy 4:40)?[9]

• All relationships (Galatians 5:13,14)?[10]

10. How has your perspective on life and on your marriage changed since you laid yourself on the altar before God?

Judy's story: I love bicycling, and one day stands out in particular. Sweat rolled down my face and into my eyes that bright afternoon as I laboriously pumped my bike up a steep incline. Climbing that hill had required months of discipline, training, and perseverance. For a long time, I had wondered if I could ever conquer this particular hill. Now, after a long arduous climb, I had finally reached the peak. However, cruising back down the slope demanded no effort whatsoever.

Living the Spirit-controlled life is like pedaling up that hill. To stay in a right relationship with God and with others requires the constant practice of confession and transparent repentance. To conquer sin and temptation require the constant practice of living from the inside out.

But when we sit back and begin to "cruise" through life, we immediately begin rolling down the hill called "backsliding," hardening our hearts toward God and building walls in our relationships with others. It's very easy to become complacent, like the people in the Laodicean church. The Lord warned them, *"I know your deeds, that you are neither cold nor hot; I would that you were cold or hot. So because you are lukewarm, and neither hot nor cold, I will spit you out of My mouth"* (Revelation 3:15,16). He also warns, *"And I will punish the men who are stagnant in spirit, who say in their hearts, 'The Lord will not do good or evil!'"* (Zephaniah 1:12). Wow! God obviously hates spiritual inertia in a person's life!

Although dying on the altar daily and walking victoriously over sin may be challenging, *"His divine power has granted to us everything pertaining to life and godliness"* (2 Peter 1:3). We don't have to choose to sin anymore!

Prayer Time

It is important for your group members to pray for each other as they grow in their understanding of living the Spirit-controlled life. Divide the group into pairs. Try to pair up each woman with someone she is not as familiar with so that your group will not split into cliques.

Have each partner pray for the other's commitment to lay herself on God's altar. Also, pray specifically for difficult areas she may be experiencing. Encourage the partners to write prayer concerns in their books (with the person's initials only) so that they can remember to pray for one another during the week.

Discussion Guide
Week Four Conversation

Opening Discussion

Developing a consistent, daily Quiet Time with God is essential for spiritual growth and for building a good marriage. Within your group, discuss what effect having a Bible study and daily Bible reading and prayer time has had on various members' personal spiritual growth over the past several weeks. Encourage members to describe particular situations where having a Quiet Time made a difference.

Discussion Time

(Note: **Instructions for you as facilitator are in bold type.** Material to say aloud during group time is in regular type. Material included in boxes is extra material to use during the discussion time if you desire.)

1. What is the result of taking our tendency to sin lightly and not recognizing our totally fallen nature?

   Proverbs 26:12 warns us about thinking we are okay on our own. **Read the verse.** We desperately need time in God's presence in order to transform us every single day!

2. What is the result of truly believing you have no good apart from Christ's Spirit within you, and that apart from His work through you, you can do nothing of eternal value?

3. What did you learn from the illustrations of Eric Liddell, Stottler, and Esther about being available to God for His purposes at any moment?

Mary and her sister Martha loved the Lord Jesus, and Mary always hung on His words, remaining spiritually sensitive. She evidently understood and believed Jesus' predictions of His death, because Mary took the one opportunity available to anoint His body for burial by pouring very costly perfume upon Him. She never had another chance to anoint Jesus' body because when the women later came to the tomb, it was empty. Jesus highly commended Mary's actions when He said, *"Truly I say to you, wherever this gospel is preached in the whole world, what this woman has done shall also be spoken of in memory of her"* (Matthew 26:13). That was her moment.

4. **Have a volunteer read 2 Corinthians 12:9,10.** According to 2 Corinthians 12:9,10, God uses our weaknesses to His glory. How have you found this to be true in your life?

5. What did you learn about the reliability and trustworthiness of God's Word, even when the world's events seem contradictory?

6. How can treasuring God's Word in your heart (Psalm 119:11) make a difference in your daily life?

Judy writes: If we let it, God's Word truly does convict and transform our lives. Many years ago, jealousy toward my brother Steve consumed my soul. Having allowed jealousy to fester inside me, it produced anger, resentment, and bitterness. One day I read James 3:16: *"Where jealousy and selfish ambition exist, there is disorder and every evil thing."* God's Word pierced my heart and convicted me of this consuming poison I had allowed in my life.

So I decided to see what the Bible taught about jealousy. Using an exhaustive concordance, I listed all the verses containing "jealous" or "jealousy," then wrote them out on a piece of paper. I saw that not only did jealousy produce *"disorder and every evil thing,"* but the real clincher came when I read that the Pharisees crucified Christ *because of jealousy* (Mark 15:10)! The same poisonous attitude in me was what killed my Lord! Then and there I confessed my sin and chose to never again allow that kind of destructive force in my life. Oh, the blessed conviction of God's Word!

7. Why is "Dying" (laying your life on the altar) such an important way to start your time in prayer?

Judy tells of her experience: How quickly we can crawl off the altar! Sometimes in the middle of the day Stottler will suggest that we pray over a decision, and periodically my internal response is, "I don't *feel* like praying!" Instantly, flashing red warning lights erupt inside me: "Warning! Warning! Brick laying in process!" My response reveals a brick of rebellion within me that doesn't want to be humbled to seek the Lord's will. I would rather make my *own* choices without "interference" from the Almighty. Thus, I have once again begun construction on a wall of pride and rebellion between me and the Lord.

It's so silly! Why wouldn't I want to pray and seek the One who gives wisdom for every decision? Why wouldn't I eagerly seek God's will, knowing that it always results in what is best for me? So whenever I sense that tiny inner resistance, I again quickly choose to crucify my pride and crawl back up on His altar.

8. What does unconfessed sin do to your intimacy with God?

9. How can wearing the armor of God each day make a difference in your responses to daily temptations?

The beginning of the Ephesians 6 passage says, *"Take up the full armor of God, that you may be able to resist in the evil day"* (v.13). The logical antithesis is that if we don't take up the armor, then we won't be able to resist when temptations come. *"For though we walk in the flesh, we do not war according to the flesh, for the weapons of our warfare are not of the flesh, but divinely powerful for the destruction of fortresses"* (2 Corinthians 10:3,4). God has provided the armor that covers us from head to toe. All we have to do is pick it up, put it on, and walk in it. Then *"the battle is the Lord's"* (1 Samuel 17:47).

10. What does it mean to pray specifically? Give an example from your own life of a specific answer to a specific question you asked God.

Prayer Time

Introduce your group members to praying through Scripture. This means using words and phrases from the Bible that apply to a certain situation as you make your requests to God. The following verses can be used, or group members can also find their own favorites. Have volunteers mention a prayer request and a verse that shows how to pray for that request. Ask someone to pray for the request, using the phrases from the Bible verse in her prayer.

1 Peter 3:15—Asking God to help prepare you for witnessing about your faith.
Galatians 5:16—Obeying God in an area of temptation.
Matthew 19:26—Having hope in a difficult situation.
1 Peter 5:7—Asking God to help you stop worrying and to trust Him instead.
Psalm 51:17—Asking God to help you live in broken humility.

Discussion Guide
Week Five Conversation

Opening Discussion

Bring these materials to your group meeting: 2 clear glasses half full of sugar; a cup of dirt; spoons; powdered drink mixed with water; glasses.

Ask: How important is purity to you? How significant is it when you allow just a little impurity in your life? **Hold up one of the glasses of sugar.** Let's say that this sugar represents our purity. Right now, it's pure. We could use it for many things. Today, we'll use it to sweeten our drinks. **Give everyone a glass and pour each person some unsweetened powdered drink.** The drink you have is unsweetened. I'll pass around the sugar so that you can add as much as you like. But first, I'm going to add an ingredient to the sugar. I'm sure you won't mind. **Spoon in several heaping spoonsful of dirt into the sugar and stir. Hand the sugar glass to the first person in the group.** How do you feel about this sugar now? Do you want any of it in your drink? No, because it has lost its purity. **Bring out the second glass of sugar. Pass it around, allowing people to spoon sugar into their drinks. While they do this, compare the sugar's purity to our purity. Discuss how purity and integrity are related.**

Discussion Time

(Note: **Instructions for you as facilitator are in bold type.** Material to say aloud during group time is in regular type. Material included in boxes is extra material to use during the discussion time if you desire.)

1. What are the three elements of obedience? Share examples from your own life or from the Bible that illustrate each of these three elements.

2. The motivations for obedience are: trust, protection from sin, blessings and rewards, and how it affects others. How do these motivate your own walk with the Lord?

God loves to bless our obedience, and encourages us to seek for the reward. All through the Old Testament, we see that when the Israelites obeyed the Lord, He multiplied their blessings. Because David walked in righteousness and loved the Lord with all his heart, God blessed him with a great kingdom and an eternal lineage. Ruth, Hannah, Esther, and Elizabeth all trusted their lives to the Lord's sovereignty and received wonderful blessings.[11]

On the other hand, God warns us that *"your sins have withheld good from you"* (Jeremiah 5:25). In Joshua chapter 7 we read the story of Achan, a man caught by the lust of his eyes. He disobeyed the Lord and "secretly" took items that God had forbidden. The consequence of his actions cost him and his entire family their lives, as well as thirty-six other men! Disobedience not only affects us, but it's far-reaching effects hurt the lives of so many around us. *No act of disobedience is insignificant!*

3. Give an example of how your obedience or disobedience to God during a difficult situation affected your family's or friends' lives.

4. Discuss your understanding of why living the Spirit-controlled life and having daily time with the Lord are the two most essential elements for your life.

> Judy says: Attempting to have daily quiet times without living the Spirit-controlled life surely leads to failure because only the Spirit can transform our actions moment by moment. Equally as disastrous is attempting to live a Spirit-controlled life without daily Quiet Times because we cannot understand God's will without time in His Word. Leading up to my time in the Caribbean, I thought I could live the Spirit-controlled life without having His daily input. But without His Word correcting and training me in righteousness, my heart quickly hardened and I slid into sin.

5. Why is it so important to gauge our behavior against the example of Christ rather than against that of other people?

6. What does this statement mean in your marriage: "Integrity begins at home"?

7. **Read Luke 16:10.** How have you found Luke 16:10 to be true in your life?

It's so much easier to "play Christian" by going to church and speaking "Christianese," rather than living lives of complete holiness. What about the other six days of the week when we speed down the road, exaggerate in conversations, live with pride and anger, pour filth into our minds through the TV, and then wonder why God doesn't bless us? The Israelites tried the same approach. But listen to God's response. **Read Jeremiah 7:9,10.**

God owns our lives 24 hours a day, 365 days a year, and He calls us to holiness and integrity in every facet. He specifically says to *"wash your heart from evil"* (Jeremiah 4:14) and to *"guard, through the Holy Spirit who dwells in us, the treasure which has been entrusted to you"* (2 Timothy 1:14).

8. **Have two volunteers read Matthew 16:24 and Romans 14:7,8.** How do these verses form the foundation for our decisions of integrity and purity?

9. **Read Psalm 101:2–4.** What guidelines on behavior do you find in this Scripture passage?

10. **Have someone read Ephesians 5:3,4.** If we actually practiced Ephesians 5:3,4, what might change in our entertainment choices?

We cannot justify watching movies that contain sexual scenes and impure or suggestive language because we believe the quality plots and overall values in those films overshadow the impurities. God doesn't give us an "exception clause" to His call for purity! He tells us to *"know no evil"* (Psalm 101:4, emphasis added).

11. How has dealing with your area(s) of media temptation made a difference in your walk with the Lord? In your marriage?

Prayer Time

Some of your group members may be struggling with bad habitual media practices or issues of obedience to something God has shown them. Use your prayer time to encourage each other in the battle for purity and complete obedience. Divide into pairs (the same pairs as the other week if possible). If they feel comfortable doing so, have partners share their difficulties in these areas with each other. Have partners pray for each other's spiritual strength to break bad media habits and to obey God in all that He shows them. Encourage pairs to become accountability partners over the next week. Remind them again that all personal information that is shared must be held in the strictest of confidence.

Discussion Guide
Week Six Conversation

Opening Discussion

Discuss how the qualities of God's love should be evident in our marital relationships. Talk about what would change in marriage vows if couples understood the qualities of His love. Then as a group, write a short set of wedding vows that reflect biblical love. (You could divide your members into smaller groups and have each write a set of vows. Then reconvene as a large group and have small groups share their vows with the other women. Remember not to take too long so that you'll have time to complete the discussion questions.)

Discussion Time

(Note: **Instructions for you as facilitator are in bold type.** Material to say aloud during group time is in regular type. Material included in boxes is extra material to use during the discussion time if you desire.)

1. **Read 1 Corinthians 13:4–7.** Which instruction in these verses is the hardest for you to practice in your marriage? Why?

2. Give an example of demonstrating love based on feelings. Then give an example of the effect 1 Corinthians 13 love can have. (The examples can be from your own life or from another woman's marriage who will remain unidentified.)

   Feelings come and go. They are incredibly fickle and unreliable. And if we begin to feel "love" toward someone other than our spouse, we can know that those feelings will someday waver as well. As we've seen from God's Word, demonstrating His love has no connection to our feelings. Godly love is one of sacrifice and selflessness, putting others before ourselves. Although it requires constant practice, we *can* demonstrate the godly love of 1 Corinthians 13 toward our spouse, as well as others around us—but only by the strength and work of Christ through us.

3. **Have a volunteer read Philippians 2:3–8.** What do you find in this Scripture passage that you can apply to the way you should relate to your husband?

4. Why is asking and giving forgiveness so hard for us? What are the results of doing so, or not doing so?

5. How do you take negative thoughts captive in a situation where your husband's behavior irks you and he has no intention of changing? (**Emphasize the process of spiritual breathing and the Spirit-controlled life. Use an example from your own life.**)

6. What is the difference between giving up your rights out of love and becoming a door mat in your marriage relationship? (**Emphasize the need to live sacrificially as well as to address issues that are harmful to the marriage relationship.**)

The secret to maintaining the right balance is to do everything for the health of your marriage. When that is your goal, you will be better able to distinguish between what you should give up and the areas in which you should stand firm. Just giving in all the time is not healthy for your marriage. Neither is selfishly hanging onto your rights for the sake of your pride. Ask the Lord for wisdom and seek godly counsel when you face confusion over how to handle some area.

7. How does practicing each of the fruits of the Spirit found in Galatians 5:22,23 make a difference in our home atmosphere, in our children's lives, and in the watching world? (**Go through each fruit separately, giving examples.**)

Because Christ's selfless, sacrificial love is so foreign to anything we see and hear in the world around us, we must depend moment by moment upon Christ to demonstrate His love through us, regardless of what our wildly vacillating emotions cry out for us to do. Those around us desperately need to see His love in action, lived through us, for we are told that His love is what sets us apart. Christ says, *"By this all men will know that you are My disciples, if you have love for one another"* (John 13:35). We don't want Christ's godly love to become the dinosaur of the American church—historical stories with no living examples!

8. Why is the principle found in Nehemiah 13:15–21 about closing the door on opportunities for sin so important for our marriages?

9. What examples did you give to begin caring for your marriage in these areas?

- Identifying my unmet needs (Song of Solomon 6:3).
- Spending exclusive time with my husband (Song of Solomon 7:10).
- Caring about my appearance (Song of Solomon 2:14).
- Laughing together (Philippians 4:4).
- Acting like a duck (Philippians 4:6,7).
- Harboring no unresolved anger against my husband (Ephesians 4:26,27).
- Praying together with my husband (Matthew 18:20).

Judy writes: It's so easy to unconsciously expect our husband to meet all our needs. But when we look to our spouse to fulfill every area of our lives, we invite disaster. If I become increasingly disillusioned with Stottler because he fails to fulfill every part of my life, then I place myself in the vulnerable position of thinking some other man could better meet my needs. For instance, if I subconsciously allow myself to be discontent with Stottler because he continually sings off key and he cannot share my deep love of music, then I suddenly become vulnerable to the next understanding male musician who crosses my path. But if I continually focus on thanking God for all of Stottler's wonderful traits, as well as thanking Him by faith for Stottler's lack of musical ability, then I safeguard my marriage. And I allow *God* to fulfill my musical needs. He created music, and He gave me those abilities. He can certainly fulfill my needs!

10. How are you going to make sure that your relationship with God and then your relationship with your husband are the two highest priorities of your life?

11. What difference might this make in the lives of your children and those close to you?

Prayer Time

Pray through 1 Corinthians 13:4–7 in this way: Read each verse or portion of a verse, then pause to let volunteers offer a prayer for their own marriages that are linked to the concept in that verse.

Discussion Guide
Week Seven Conversation

Opening Discussion

(**Read these two paragraphs to the group.**) The Bible reminds us over and over that temptations will come. None of us is immune. Young believers may fall due to unfamiliarity with God's Word and lack of experience with the Spirit-controlled life. But older, more mature believers are just as vulnerable to falling because we often want to depend on our "spiritual maturity."

Satan never looks at a mature Christian and says, "Wow, her walk with the Lord is so strong that I won't bother trying to tempt her." Hardly! In fact, if anything, the stronger our testimony, the greater the victory for Satan if we fall. We must never assume that we stand above any temptation. *"Therefore let him who thinks he stands take heed that he does not fall"* (1 Corinthians 10:12). And when we realize our capacity to fall into any sin, then we wisely choose to protect ourselves by running in dependence to the Lord and also setting up accountability with others.

Have the group members discuss why accountability is so important in a marriage. If they begin debating the No Secrets Policy, ask them to wait on that discussion until they start into the questions below.

Discussion Time

(Note: **Instructions for you as facilitator are in bold type.** Material to say aloud during group time is in regular type. Material included in boxes is extra material to use during the discussion time if you desire.)

Dr. Willard Harley writes "Either honesty is always right, or you'll always have an excuse for being dishonest."[12]

1. Why is it so hard to be honest with your marriage partner in some areas?

As we talked about earlier, to fully experience God's design of becoming "one flesh" emotionally and spiritually, we must have no lies, secrets, or deceit separating us from our spouse. And if we haven't established the pattern of the No Secrets Policy in our marriage *before* a temptation, it's a given that we won't choose to start once the emotional allure toward another man has gripped our heart! God's Word tells us that He desires *"truth in the innermost being"* (Psalm 51:6). But our fallen nature constantly seeks to find excuses, such as, "Surely God doesn't want me to hurt my husband by telling him about some past indiscretion."

Such excuses won't work before God. For one, if we've been unfaithful, we've *already* hurt our spouse because of our infidelity and the ensuing lies to hide the truth. For another, it's not really our husband we're trying to protect—it's ourselves! And on top of that, if we've been unfaithful once (or more) and have "gotten away with it," we're far more likely to fall again when a desirable temptation lures our heart away.

As we look at the lives of Achan (Joshua 7), Jonah (Jonah 1), and Ananias and Sapphira (Acts 5:1-11), to name a few, we see that God has given us ample illustrations of the consequences of lack of honesty. Therefore, we must obey God and what He calls us to do rather than allow the fear of our mate's response to hinder our obedience. Whatever God calls us to do, He gives us the grace to carry out. Of course, we must *always* share difficult things with the sensitivity of the Lord, speaking from a heart broken over our sin.

2. Which quality of accountability (being teachable, vulnerable, honest, dependable) is the most difficult for you? Why?

3. How does spending time in God's Word help you build walls of protection in your marriage?

4. **Read 2 Samuel 11:1–4.** In these verses, how did David violate the principles of the Spirit-controlled life and accountability taught in *The Enticement of the Forbidden*?

5. What are some practical ways we can safeguard ourselves from getting involved in improper relationships with other men?

6. **Read 1 Timothy 2:9,10.** How does 1 Timothy 2:9,10 apply to women today? Why is this important?

7. What are some practical ways we can guard our eyes and ears?

8. How can e-mails and chat rooms pose a threat to a marriage?

The harm of a secret Internet relationship on a marriage is very real. Secrecy in marriage *always* brings damage. It creates an emotional separation between the couple and builds barriers to overcome. Private Internet conversations deny the spouse the intimacy that should have been theirs. And even if on-line conversations remain platonic and spiritual in nature, when the Internet relationship begins consuming time and energy that should have been given to the marriage, their mates are deprived and the boundary line has been crossed.

Take heed! For a married woman, any long or frequent "conversations" over the Internet with another man create an enormous breach in the wall of protection around your marriage. It becomes far too easy to pour your heart out to this faceless individual in some weak moment.

9. How are you doing on accountability with your husband and with another woman in order to protect your marriage?

I (Judy) cannot overemphasize how the No Secrets Policy acts as one of our greatest forms of marital protection. Please do not treat this lightly or brush it off as too difficult. With one in every three to four married women becoming involved in some form of infidelity, we *must* build fortresses of protection around our marriages!

10. What are some creative and fun ways you can spend more time with your husband?

As we practice building the walls of protection around our marriages, we could become the generation that reduces the statistics of divorce within the church! By God's grace and wisdom, we can do it!

Prayer Time

Ask volunteers to mention areas where their walls of protection are weak. When someone mentions an area, have another group member pray for it right away. Then ask for another volunteer. Continue in this pattern until everyone who wants to has had a chance to give a request and receive prayer. Remind them again that all information and prayer requests are to remain in the strictest of confidence.

Discussion Guide
Week Eight Conversation

Opening Discussion

Use this time to help the women evaluate what they have learned through the Bible study times. Ask what stood out in their lives from the "Evaluating My Views" section in Lesson 5. Then have volunteers share their responses to the question found in Lesson 5: "The most important step(s) I am taking to build and protect my marriage is. . ."

Discussion Time

(Note: **Instructions for you as facilitator are in bold type.** Material to say aloud during group time is in regular type. Material included in boxes is extra material to use during the discussion time if you desire.)

1. After going through this study, what is your attitude now toward the statement: "Never underestimate the power of attraction"?

The eight things we must not do when attracted to another man are:
    1. Don't divulge your feelings.
    2. Don't keep secrets.
    3. Don't be lured in by the adrenaline rush.
    4. Don't give in to curiosity.
    5. Don't flirt.
    6. Don't fantasize.
    7. Don't give in to rescue tendencies.
    8. Don't doubt Scripture or God.

2. Which of these is your weakest area? What will you do to counteract your weakness?

3. What are some scenarios in which you could find yourself vulnerable in these areas? What predetermined boundaries have you set to guard against these situations?

Have you ever dreamed about another man and then considered telling him? Does your heart desire to further a relationship with another man, and you look forward to telling him exciting things that should instead be shared with your husband? Do you wonder what it would be like to sit and chat with some friendly gentleman over coffee? Do you ever say to yourself, "I may be curious about what it's like to spend time with this man, but of course I would never have an affair!"?

The very fact that you are toying with the sin in the first place reveals that your heart actually *does* desire this temptation. And God says that "*the devising of folly is sin*" (Proverbs 24:9). Even to *dwell* on the possibility of sharing such things with another man is to have crossed over from temptation into disobedience and sin. Those predetermined boundaries are so important!

4. The Seven Immediate Steps for Responding to Marital Temptation are crucial for waging spiritual battle. How do you see these seven steps making a critical difference in your victory over sin if drawn toward another man?

Doing "whatever it takes" may mean confronting some difficult choices. One married high-ranking woman in the military has a job that frequently requires her to be separated from her family for long periods of time. Because she continually must live and work in such close contact with brave men in uniform, she repeatedly struggles with attraction to her coworkers. To leave at this point in her career would be to lose all her retirement benefits. But what is it worth to gain prestige and a solid retirement if you've lost your family?

If your job or your position puts you around enticing men who cause you to continually struggle with purity, God says to flee. That may mean quitting a job, changing churches, or moving to another town or state. But if our priorities are right—God, husband, family, job—then the choice is clear. God will honor our sacrifices made for the sake of righteousness and purity. In the perspective of eternity, what can be more important than obeying God and walking in holiness?

5. What principles for resisting temptation did you find in Proverbs 1:10, Proverbs 4:14,15; Psalm 86:7; Romans 6:12,13 (in Lesson 3)? **Read each passage and discuss each separately.**

6. **Have two volunteers read 2 Corinthians 4:17 and 2 Timothy 4:7,8.** What kind of motivation to remain faithful in the battle do you find in these passages?

7. What do the following verses say about a godly wife? **Read each passage and discuss.**

   • Proverbs 18:22
   • Proverbs 19:14
   • Proverbs 31:10,11

8. **Read Proverbs 31:26–30.** How do verses 26–29 describe a godly wife? What contrast do we find in verse 30?

9. What did God lead you to write for a mission statement in Lesson 5? How will your light shine before others so that they will see a changed life, one pointing to the miraculous, transforming work of Jesus Christ?

Prayer Time

Divide your group into prayer partners. Then say: "Whether your husband is a godly man or you struggle in a difficult marriage, God wants to fill your life with faith so that you can experience His fullness and joy. Your decisions make all the difference. If you determine to cling to the Lord, then He can give you His peace and joy no matter what your circumstances may be."

Have prayer partners give every good and every difficult aspect of their marriages to God. Ask Him to work in the challenging areas. Then have partners thank God by faith that He is always in control and that "*the Lord is good to all and His mercies are over all His works*" (Psalm 145:9).

Then have them thank Him for the specific work He has done in their lives these past eight weeks. Thank Him for the work He has yet to do and that He "*who began a good work in you will carry it on to completion until the day of Christ Jesus*" (Philippians 1:6, NIV).

End your prayer time with praise, for "*who is like You, majestic in holiness, awesome in praise, working wonder?*" (Exodus 15:11).

"Holy and awesome is His name" (Psalm 111:9).

Notes

Personal Study, Week 1

1. Dr. Willard F. Harley, Jr., "A Summary of Dr. Harley's Basic Concepts," February 19, 2003, <www.marriagebuilders.com/graphic/mbi3550_summary.html>.
2. Dr. James C. Dobson, *Love Must Be Tough* (Nashville, TN: Thomas Nelson, Inc., 1996), 227. Quoting *Psychology Today*, 1983.
3. Ibid, 156.
4. Susan T. Foh, *Women and the Word of God: A Response to Biblical Feminism* (Phillipsburg, N.J.: Presbyterian and Reformed Publishing Co., 1979), 186. Quoted by Cynthia Heald, *Loving Your Husband*, (Colorado Springs, CO: NavPress, 1989), 61.
5. Mike Mason, *The Mystery of Marriage* (Sisters, OR: Multnomah Books, 1985), 58.
6. Charles Colson, "Marital Safety Nets: Community Marriage Policies," BreakPoint with Charles Colson, commentary #020225, February 25, 2002, February 28, 2002, <www.breakpoint.org>.
7. Christine A. Johnson, Scott M. Stanley, Norval D. Glenn, Paul R. Amato, Steve L. Nock, Howard J. Markman, M. Robin Dion, "Marriage in Oklahoma: 2001 Baseline Statewide Survey on Marriage and Divorce, a Project of the Oklahoma Marriage Initiative," Oklahoma State University Bureau for Social Research, 2001, March 26, 2004, <www.okmarriage.org>, 2.
8. Shirley Glass, "Shattered Vows," *Psychology Today* (July/August, 1998). August 21, 2002, <www.findarticles.com/cf_dls/m1175/n4_v31/20845729/print.jhtml>.
9. Avis Gunther-Rosenberg, "A Marriage Guru Looks at Unfaithful," *Providence Journal* (May 15, 2002): G7, G12.

Personal Study, Week 2

1. See John 10:10; 14:27; Galatians 5:22,23 for extra insight.
2. See Romans 2:4; 2 Timothy 2:24–26; Romans 1:24; Proverbs 29:1; Proverbs 1:28–33; James 5:19,20 for extra insight.
3. Cynthia Heald, *Loving Your Husband* (Colorado Springs, CO: NavPress, 1989), 7.
4. Dr. Joyce Brothers, "Family Secrets: Handle With Care," *Parade Magazine* (September 7, 2003): 4.

Personal Study, Week 3

1. Used with permission from Tim St.Clair, Life Action Ministries, October 2003.
2. "Clear Conscience" pamphlet, Life Action Ministries, January 1, 2000 <www.lifeaction.org/Articles/viewarticle.asp?id=1031103317>.
3. Bill Bright, "Sin On Ice," *Worldwide Challenge* (May/June 2002): 46.
4. *The Wycliffe Bible Commentary*, ed. by Charles F. Pfeiffer, Everett F. Harrison (Chicago: Moody Press, 1981), 1296.
5. C.S. Lewis, *The Joyful Christian* (New York: Macmillan Publishing Company, 1977), 141.

Personal Study, Week 4

1. Used by permission from Warren Wiersbe.
2. Andrew Murray, *With Christ in the School of Prayer* (Old Tappan, N.J.: Fleming H. Revell Co., 1965), 124.

Personal Study, Week 6

1. Dr. Bill Bright, "Insights from Bill Bright, Reflections from the Founder of Campus Crusade for Christ," October 30, 2002, November 11, 2002 <www.crosswalk.com/faith/>.
2. Sir Winston Spenser Churchill, First Statement as Prime Minister, House of Commons, May 13, 1940. Quoted in *Familiar Quotations*, by John Bartlett, 14th edition (Boston, MA: Little, Brown & Co., 1968), 921.
3. Charles R. Swindoll, *Strike the Original Match* (Portland, OR: Multnomah Press, 1980), 165. Quoted by Cynthia Heald, *Loving Your Husband* (Colorado Springs, CO: NavPress, 1989), 107.

Personal Study, Week 7

1. Paul Hattaway, *The Heavenly Man* (London: Monarch Books, 2002), 14.
2. Dr. Willard F. Harley, Jr., "Coping with Infidelity: Part 2, How Should Affairs End?" February 29, 2003, <www.marriagebuilders.com/graphic/mbi5060_qa.html>.
3. Rebecca Valentine, "Amidst the Storm," *Worldwide Challenge* (May/June 2001): 37.
4. Charles R. Swindoll, *Living Above the Level of Mediocrity: A Commitment to Excellence* (Waco, TX: Word Books, 1987), 123.

Personal Study, Week 8

1. "Clear Conscience" pamphlet, Life Action Ministries, January 1, 2000 <www.lifeaction.org/Articles/viewarticles.asp?id=1031103317>.

Discussion Guide

1. Dennis Rainey, *Staying Close* (Dallas, TX: Word Publishing, 1989), 81.
2. Dr. Willard F. Harley, Jr., "Coping with Infidelity: Part 2, How Should Affairs End?" February 29, 2003, <www.marriagebuilders.com/graphic/mbi5060_qa.html>.
3. Tom Neven, "The Work of His Hands," *Focus on the Family* (March 2001): 7.
4. Susan Graham Mathis, "One Amazing Lady: Kay Coles James," *Focus on the Family* (October/November 2003): 5.
5. Also see Romans 6:6,12,13; Romans 8:5–9,12–14; John 6:63; Galatians 2:20; 5:16,17,24,25; 6:7–9; 2 Corinthians 10:3,4; 1 John 2:16,17.
6. Also see Ephesians 4:22–24; Philippians 4:7,8; Romans 12:2; Colossians 3:2; 1 Corinthians 2:16; 2 Corinthians 11:3; Matthew 22:37,38; Psalm 26:2; Proverbs 12:5; Isaiah 26:3; 1 Peter 1:13.
7. Also see Colossians 3:16,17; Psalm 40:3; Proverbs 8:7; 10:32; Matthew 12:34; Luke 6:45.
8. Also see Proverbs 12:4; 19:14; 5:18; Titus 2:3–5; 1 Peter 3:1–6; Ephesians 5:22-33; Colossians 3:18; 1 Corinthians 7:2–5,10-16; Hebrews 13:4; Malachi 2:13-16; Romans 7:2,3; Mark 10:11,12; Matthew 19:3–9.
9. Also see Jeremiah 32:38,39; Psalm 90:16; Acts 2:38,39.
10. Also see Matthew 22:39; John 13:34; 15:17; Romans 12:10; 13:8,10; 1 Corinthians 16:14; Ephesians 5:1,2; Colossians 3:14; 1 Thessalonians 3:12; 4:9; 1 Peter 4:8; 1 John 3:11; 4:7,11.
11. See Ruth; 1 Samuel 1:1,2,11,19,20; Esther; Luke 1:5–25,57–66.
12. Dr. Willard F. Harley, Jr., "A Summary of Dr. Harley's Basic Concepts" <www.marriagebuilders.com/graphic/mbi3550_summary.html>.